AUGUSTINE'S OAK

Peter Oswald

AUGUSTINE'S OAK

OBERON BOOKS
LONDON

First published in 1999 by Oberon Books Ltd.
(incorporating Absolute Classics)
521 Caledonian Road, London N7 9RH
Tel: 020 7607 3637 / Fax: 020 7607 3629
e-mail: oberon.books@btinternet.com

Reprinted with corrections, 1999

ISBN 1 84002 128 4

Cover design: Andrzej Klimowski

Typography: Richard Doust

Cover photograph: Tom McShane

Author photograph: John Timbers

Printed in Great Britain by MPG Books Ltd, Cornwall.

Characters

AUGUSTINE

LAURENCE

ALBANUS

SEVERUS

PAULINUS

KING ETHELBERT OF KENT

QUEEN BERTHA

TATA
their daughter

EDWIN
Prince of Deira

ATHELSTAN

OSBERT

PAGAN PRIESTS

LILLA

EUMER
an assassin

BISHOP OF ST DAVID'S

BISHOP OF ELWY

DINOTH
Abbot of Bangor

ANEIRIN
a bard

OLWEN
a prophetess

AN ANGEL

A WESSEX WOMAN

A MAID

MIDWIFE

MESSENGER

LORDS

LOKI
a god

WODEN
a god

FREYA
a goddess

Augustine's Oak was first performed at the Globe on 6 August 1999 with the following cast:

AUGUSTINE, Terry McGinity
LAURENCE, Harry Gostelow
ALBANUS, Paul Chahidi
SEVERUS, Jan Knightley
PAULINUS, Robert Pickavance
ETHELBERT, Martin Turner
BERTHA, Yolanda Vazquez
TATA, Philippa Stanton
EDWIN, Sean O'Callaghan
ATHELSTAN, Vincenzo Nicoli
OSBERT, Richard Trahair
PAGAN PRIESTS, Avril Clark, Marcello Magni,
    Robert Pickavance
LILLA, Marcello Magni
EUMER, Jan Knightley
BISHOP OF ST DAVID'S, Richard Trahair
BISHOP OF ELWY, Vincenzo Nicoli
DINOTH, Harry Gostelow
ANEIRIN, Leader Hawkins
OLWEN, Jules Melvin
AN ANGEL, Avril Clark
A WESSEX WOMAN, Avril Clark
LOKI, Paul Chahidi
WODEN, Robert Pickavance
FREYA, Avril Clark
WARRIORS, Jan Knightley, Vincenzo Nicoli
MAIDS TO TATA, Avril Clark, Jules Melvin
NORTHUMBRIAN PRIEST, Paul Chahidi
SACRIFICIAL VICTIM, Richard Trahair
NORTHUMBRIANS, Avril Clark, Harry Gostelow,
    Jan Knightley, Jules Melvin, Terry McGinity,
    Vincenzo Nicoli
LORDS, Vincenzo Nicoli, Richard Trahair

Acknowledgements

All plays are collaborations, this one especially so. It was commissioned by Mark Rylance, the artistic director of the Globe in 1996. Mark applied for an Arts Council bursary and from June 1998 to June 1999, I was the writer in residence at the Globe. It was Mark's vision that there should be a new play at the Globe. He supported it throughout, working in a triumverate with the director, Tim Carroll, and myself on the script I came up with. This was later thrown open to the cast, and there is something of each of them in it too. The whole atmosphere at the Globe is one of encouragement and excitement, but I would especially like to thank Greg Ripley-Duggan and Claire van Kampen for theirs.

For Alice.

ACT ONE

Scene 1

Britain. Enter ANEIRIN.

ANEIRIN: Oh why did the disciple when his Lord
                                   had risen
  Embark with Mary for this prehistoric country
  Beyond the bloody end? And why did Constantine
  Rally his men for Rome in Britain, the divine,
  The far away, whose hills are mounds of kings piled
                                   high
  On mounds of kings and tombs of gods and giant men?
  Where is the Holy Grail? Where is it to be found,
  And where is Arthur sleeping under the green rain?
  Great God is in this country waiting to be found,
  An old drunk thrown out, an old travelling man.
  The Pope of Rome was walking in his holy garden
  And heard the moon and sun singing about this island;
  Of how the King of Kent is pagan and his wife
  Christian – not a good basis for a quiet marriage,
  But a God-given moment for a papal mission.

  Exit.

Scene 2

The court of King Ethelbert of Kent in Canterbury. BERTHA is praying, in mourning. Enter ETHELBERT.

ETHELBERT: My love, the horses are ready.

BERTHA: I'm just coming.

ETHELBERT: You don't have to if you don't want to.

BERTHA: No, I'm just coming.

ETHELBERT: Well, stay then.

BERTHA: What?

ETHELBERT: You are in mourning, my heart. He was your chaplain – stay and grieve –

BERTHA: But I said I wanted to come.

ETHELBERT: It's just a question of when.

BERTHA: Well, I may not be moving as quickly as usual.

ETHELBERT: Then stay, stay!

BERTHA: You think I'll spoil it?

ETHELBERT: No!

BERTHA: If I come slowly can I still come?

ETHELBERT: We will wait for you until hell eats heaven!

BERTHA: Alright, I won't come.

ETHELBERT: Oh please!

BERTHA: No!

ETHELBERT: Alright, don't!

BERTHA: I won't! I never had any intention –

ETHELBERT: Well, you've wasted half the day – twelve men waiting on a cold spring morning –

BERTHA: What, the ones who'd wait till hell eats heaven?

ETHELBERT: Hell has eaten heaven!

BERTHA: What do you mean?

ETHELBERT: I mean you've made me shout at you, my dear, when you're in mourning, and now I must go out without you, furious.

BERTHA: But we will be friends again, this evening!

ETHELBERT: Agony!

BERTHA: As it is, you have made it impossible for me
    to accompany you on an important event.

ETHELBERT: I begged you to come!

BERTHA: As long as I ran! But I am in mourning!
    I should be praying at his graveside, I have forsaken
    that! It will never come again!

ETHELBERT: Ah Woden!

*He runs out. BERTHA hides her face in her hands, laughing
and crying. Enter TATA.*

BERTHA: Tata my dear, this priest was hesitant,
    And he is dead now; learn a lesson from him.
    How can we save your father from the pit?
    Although I love him, he could die tonight
    And follow Woden straight to Satan's throne.

TATA: How can we help him?

BERTHA: Find another chaplain!
    One who will speak more boldly to your father.
    Meanwhile, continue to misunderstand him.

TATA: How will that help? Will it encourage him
    To understand you?

BERTHA: Stand up straight, my darling.
    I need your help now. For the first ten years
    I tried to teach him what was taught to me,
    And he seemed open and intent to learn.
    But never quite entirely taken over.
    And I began to see that all the time
    My husband had been cunningly delaying
    His understanding, to prolong the lesson.
    For his soul's sake I have reversed our roles,
    And for ten years I have been cold and backward –

Which is extremely difficult for me
Because as time went on I found I missed him –
So here we are, both longing for each other,
In the same house, as far apart as planets.

TATA: You love my father? And you have pretended
For all these years, and brought me up believing
That wives and husbands tolerate each other.

BERTHA: My heart is like a robin on his thumb,
But for the love of Christ I am an eagle.
Tata beware!

TATA: Beware what?

BERTHA: Everything!
How will you find your way across the world
From birth to death and keep your heart unbroken?
Can't do it!

TATA: Then I might as well not worry.

BERTHA: You should begin to worry slightly now
So as to keep from having to be worried
A great deal later. You are nearly twenty;
None of the princes in this land is Christian.
I was a prize beyond your father's dreams –
To get the daughter of the King of Paris,
Was, for the King of Kent, quite fortunate;
You are the daughter of the King of Kent,
Therefore, not worth much on the continent.
So think how you, a Christian from the womb,
Will cope with being married to a pagan,
As I have had to. Watch your mother now,
In case she dies or goes insane tomorrow.

TATA: Why should my husband have to be a Christian?
Are Christians braver? Are they better-smelling?

BERTHA: Tata, I know these gods and goddesses
Like my own nightmares – all my married life

I have had Woden farting in the bathroom
Or that fat Freya crammed into my wardrobe,
These images surround me, I have almost
Grown fond of them; and lately they have changed;
Freya is fading, she is old and thin,
Mad Woden now is all they talk about,
Woden who wishes the whole world was fighting.

TATA: Well, if they want him we can't stop them.

BERTHA: Listen!
I want my husband and I want him Christian!
Can I allow the man I love to die
Into the arms of Satan? I will fight.
There is a kind of mystery between us,
We are still curious about each other;
It is unheard of for a king and queen
To take the slightest notice of each other –
But there, the world is coming to an end,
And everything is changing for the better!
And I still want to tie him in a bundle
Of thoughts, and have him in the morning closer
Than my own bones!

TATA: Imagine if these names
Were just the drool of your imagination
And there was not just no Thor and no Woden
But no Christ, Spirit, God or Mary – nothing,
And everything sprang out of everything
For its own sake – it would be very sad
For you and he to have been so divided;
Absurd in fact –

BERTHA: The key is to agree –
And we agree he must agree with me.
Or are you more in favour of fat Freya?

TATA: I am like you!

BERTHA: Thank God! The king is coming.
I am upstairs in tears – you talk to him.

Exit BERTHA. Enter ETHELBERT.

ETHELBERT: I simply don't have the strength for this, but nor do I have the slightest choice. Love is like your own head, you can't just shrug it off. My father had six mistresses, and never argued with the queen his wife. I am paying the price for breaking with tradition.

TATA: Why have you come straight back?

ETHELBERT: The messengers of Ethelfrith turned their backs on us and rode off. That was their message. So I sent my council to catch up with them, to tell them that we feel the same.

TATA: Does King Ethelfrith want to fight?

ETHELBERT: He has killed all the other kings north of the Humber, now he feels no need to bow to me and so he says so. But we may not have to fight him, he may wake up dead one morning. Forget him.

TATA: Mama is in tears.

ETHELBERT: She is in mourning.

TATA: Oh it's far worse than that.

ETHELBERT: Yes I know what she's crying about. I have cried too, and I am the king. I thought I cried a lot when I was only the King of Kent. Then they made me the King of the Kings of Britain and I cried even more. It never stops. Perhaps it's because we live on an island, your eyes are always trying to reach the sea. There is no landscape as mountainous as a marriage.

TATA: Will you get her another chaplain?

ETHELBERT: Of course I will! But we'll never find another one like old Lethard.

TATA: He didn't do much good.

ETHELBERT: He understood me, you see. We could talk, he and I. A wonderful man, interested in everything. He talked about the things I like to talk about.

TATA: And all the time Bertha thought he was converting you.

ETHELBERT: Well yes, he was dishonest. Lethard would say to your mother, I'm going to have a bit of a chat with the king, and go off, and she'd drop to her knees and pray every instant of the time she knew he was with me; Lethard would turn up wherever I was and we'd drink and sit talking about politics or hunting almost till dawn, then when I saw her she'd say, did you have a good talk with Lethard, and I'd smile thoughtfully and reply, very interesting indeed; and she'd think I was making progress.

TATA: Now she thinks you're lost forever.

ETHELBERT: Why it should be a condition of entry to her secret heart that I believe in Jesus Christ, I can't see. I am her husband.

TATA: But couldn't you say you do?

ETHELBERT: Ah but it wouldn't be enough for me to whisper in her ear, love I believe. I'd have to be publicly baptised. And anyway it's her heart I want and I couldn't go creeping into that dressed in feathers.

TATA: Well, you're killing her.

ETHELBERT: I beg your pardon?

TATA: You're wearing her out!

ETHELBERT: Really?

TATA: Yes it's wearing her out pretending to be angry with you.

ETHELBERT: This is far too complex for a king of my race. I imagine they suffer from such intrigues in Byzantium and Paris, but with us things ought to be clear and simple.

TATA: But they're not.

ETHELBERT: Do I tear my hair out and weep because she won't believe in Woden, for heaven's sake?

TATA: No, but that's different.

ETHELBERT: Why?

TATA: Because that's all gobbledygook.

ETHELBERT: If your grandmother was here! Which she is! Ah, dear dear dear. Woden, don't listen.

TATA: He has never helped you!

ETHELBERT: But that's what he's like.

TATA: Then why don't you get him back?

ETHELBERT: You can't outwit the one-eyed one. Consider, Tata, my dear – his horse has eight legs. It takes him to the land of the dead and back in a night. He has drunk from Mimir's spring, he gave one eye in exchange for a sip; now he knows everything. He can nod to Freya and you will never have any children, your husband will lose his mind and stab you to death in bed when you are pregnant. Or he can nod to Thor and the hammer of disaster will fall smash on this kingdom, distribute our people as slaves to all comers. He can wink at Frey – close his only eye – and the wheat will wither. He can stare through the sky and on the day of battle turn me into a bird, chirping and flapping – all these things have

18

happened, and continually happen, and not without reason because, my darling, Woden, the mad one, is in command. Fear him!

TATA: (*Sings.*)
Wounded and wind-lashed on the tree,
For nine days and nine nights I hanged;
That was immortal agony –
The night fell clawed, the sun rose fanged –

Pierced by the spear, I gave my life
To Woden; Woden is my name;
I was the husband and the wife,
The gift, the giver. Who can claim

To know the darkness and the light
To which the roots and branches reach
Of the great frame that bore my weight,
Above the spring whose drops can teach

The drinker wisdom? Pinned on high,
I starved above the holy well;
On the ninth night I gave a cry,
Looked down, perceived all things, and fell.

ETHELBERT: That was my mother singing.

TATA: But this'll kill your wife. Now that her chaplain's gone she'll do nothing but fast and pray and pretend to be angry – they're obsessive, these Parisians.

ETHELBERT: I will get her another chaplain, of enormous dimensions.

TATA: Maybe that would be best.

Enter OSBERT.

OSBERT: King Ethelbert! Two monks from Rome are here to see you.

ETHELBERT: What?

OSBERT: Two monks.

ETHELBERT: Not from Gaul?

OSBERT: No, all the way from Rome.

ETHELBERT: Impossible! What are they doing here?
Rome? What do they look like?

OSBERT: Shall I show them in?

ETHELBERT: No!

TATA: Let them in!

ETHELBERT: No! No monks!

TATA: Oh! All the way from Rome!

ETHELBERT: I have my reasons.

OSBERT: They landed on Thanet. Their leader is there
now, with the rest, about forty of them.

ETHELBERT: Forty!

OSBERT: His name's Augustine. They've come all the
way from Rome to see you, King.

Enter BERTHA. ETHELBERT doesn't see her.

ETHELBERT: What do they have to come here for?
We know what we believe! This is our country, they
can't preach to us – who do they think they are?
I won't listen to them, send them away, I want no
foreign religion!

BERTHA: Oh my husband! Is this how you spoke to
Father Liudhard?

ETHELBERT: Bertha!

BERTHA: Now I know what you really think.

ETHELBERT: No you don't. My dear, Father Lethard
was one man, this Augustine has come with forty
monks, it's an invasion.

BERTHA: Oh poor King!

20

ETHELBERT: Of course I will listen to Augustine.
He may have something to say.

BERTHA: So let in his messengers!

ETHELBERT: No.

BERTHA: Have you changed your mind?

ETHELBERT: No –

BERTHA: Well, let them in!

ETHELBERT: Heaven help us!

BERTHA: How very strange you are, my husband!

ETHELBERT: I think my brain's about to burst!
Send this message to Augustine – I will come to
see him on the island of Thanet, in the open.
Osbert, would you please explain my reasons to
the queen?

Exit ETHELBERT.

BERTHA: Osbert –

OSBERT: Queen, my King Ethelbert, being very full of
ancient wisdom, is not so foolish as to be taken
unawares. He knows that the powers of wizards are
greatest indoors. Outside, under the sky, which is
ruled by Tiu, whose thunderbolts are in Thor's
hands, the king is safer.

BERTHA: Thank you, Osbert. Tata, they have come,
Christ's wizards!

Exeunt.

Scene 3

Thanet. Enter AUGUSTINE and LAURENCE, not liking the cold.

AUGUSTINE: Laurence, this place is not like Italy.

LAURENCE: It is another kind of dream, Augustine.

AUGUSTINE: A sleep without dreams. Look at all the
                          herons,
    Like scribes who stand and meditate in ponds,
    With their cloaks tucked up not to touch the water,
    And their long pens stuck sideways in their mouths;
    Or you could say grey trees bereft of leaves
    That stretch out branches weed-snagged at high tide
    Suddenly and uplift into the sky,
    As if the sky had dropped into the trees.
    Indeed, the world is upside-down in Britain,
    The British sky is like a sullen sea,
    With ranks of grey waves passing endlessly;
    I think my soul has turned to salt, the sea
    Has pushed its rhythms right into my mind,
    And oh the long drawn-out flat tragedy
    Of low tide, when the curve-billed birds come down
    To stick their heads into the mud and scream.

LAURENCE: So you don't like this country?

AUGUSTINE: Certainly!
    It is our mission. Holy Gregory
    Has given us to this and he is wise.
    These are the fringes of the soul of Britain,
    Where its heart touches the sea's desolation.
    We will pass through this. This is our beginning.
    And when the Kingdom comes, who knows, maybe
    This country will be more like Italy.

LAURENCE: Now that Augustine is in Britain, heaven
    Will not keep back the Kingdom from this island.

AUGUSTINE: I know you say this out of love for me,
    And love is something we must not refuse –
    Except that too much love can make us proud.
    I have demolished in myself a mountain
    Of pride, by spadefuls, and the work was hard.
    Be careful not to build me up too high!

LAURENCE: Severus and Albanus with a native!

Enter SEVERUS and ALBANUS with ATHELSTAN.

ALBANUS: A convert! A convert! Our first convert!

SEVERUS: His faith is magnificent!

ALBANUS: It's unbelievable – just like that! We barely
opened our mouths! If they're all like this it'll be easy
– God has gone before us – we'll have converted
Britain in a fortnight.

AUGUSTINE: What is your name?

ATHELSTAN: My name is Athelstan.

AUGUSTINE: Are you a Christian?

ATHELSTAN: Certainly I am.

AUGUSTINE: And did these men convert you?

ALBANUS: No, not us!
It was the spirit in us!

ATHELSTAN: (*Answering AUGUSTINE.*) Not exactly.

ALBANUS: I told him, God came down in human form
To earth as Jesus Christ and saved us all –
Do you believe that? And he answered, yes –

AUGUSTINE: Was this your first encounter with the
                    Word?

ATHELSTAN: Do I speak Latin?

AUGUSTINE: I can understand you.

ATHELSTAN: I learnt it from Her Majesty the Queen.
I am her servant. With the Latin language,
She also taught me Christianity.
I and a dozen others are believers,
In the king's court. And so the king chose me
To be his herald to yourselves today.

The king is coming! Yes, King Ethelbert,
Accepted as the highest king in Britain,
Is coming here to listen to your wisdom.
This is the place, right here beside the sea,
Out in the open where there are no houses.

AUGUSTINE: The judgement comes upon us suddenly!

SEVERUS: We are not ready, we need time to pray!

AUGUSTINE: Almighty Father, you have brought
us here
Across your deep, depending on your weather;
Just as from you we have the air we breathe,
So fill us with your thoughts and judgements now,
To teach the English king whose mind, to us,
Is like a tiger or some foreign flower;
Send us a sign that you are with us here.

LAURENCE: Abbott, you will be everything to him!

AUGUSTINE: Now we must fetch our banner and our
cross,
And come back calmly, chanting, in procession.

*Exeunt. Sound of a hunting horn. Enter ETHELBERT,
BERTHA, TATA, PRIEST and PRIESTESS. The
PRIEST and PRIESTESS beat drums and chant and touch
the ground with wands.*

ETHELBERT: How is the place?

PRIEST: A place of power, King. No matter what god
they serve, they cannot harm you here. On your
right hand, your own country, that belongs to Woden
your ancestor, on your left hand, the sea, from which
our people came, sacred to Frey who loves you.

ETHELBERT: Here I will take my stand, like a king.
Priests, get behind me, I don't need you!

PRIEST: Here they come!

*Enter AUGUSTINE and MONKS in procession chanting,
carrying a large silver cross and a board with a picture of*

Christ on it. They come to a halt. BERTHA and TATA rush forward and kiss AUGUSTINE.

BERTHA: Welcome to England, bearer of the Word!
I am Queen Bertha, this is Princess Tata!

ETHELBERT: This is chaos! I should address them first! Interpreter!

ATHELSTAN steps forward.

No, not you, I know what you think. Where's my man?

OSBERT steps forward.

How's your Latin?

OSBERT: Better than Caesar's!

ETHELBERT: But this is Christian Latin, Osbert, and I know you're not a Christian – yet!

OSBERT: Christian, me? (*They laugh.*) But it's the same, more or less the same.

ETHELBERT: Tell it like it is, Osbert, talk straight.

Addresses the MONKS.

Welcome back, Romans, to the land you once conquered. It's been a long time.

OSBERT: Welcome, descendants of the troops of Caesar,
To your lost province, long evacuated.

ETHELBERT: Why have you come here? What do you want to talk about? Speak plainly.

OSBERT: What is the reason for your presence here?
What are the teachings you have brought to us?
Feel free to speak directly, we are folk
Who understand unhampered language best.

AUGUSTINE: King Ethelbert, Queen Bertha,
                                councillors –
Pope Gregory, Christ's vicar to our church,

Has sent us here from Rome across the sea,
Through many dangers, overseen by demons;
What could have made us leave our native city
And strive on foot through omens of destruction
To you, except a love that comes from heaven?

OSBERT: Pope Gregory has sent them from Rome.

BERTHA: They have risked death to bring you new life!

TATA: Mother!

ETHELBERT: We have a team of interpreters. Queen,
thank you for your passion – it's a long time since
you've spoken to me in that tone!

AUGUSTINE: We do not come here as great Caesar came,
In force to conquer; we are few in number.

OSBERT: He explains that this is not a military invasion.

BERTHA: They are spiritual warriors!

TATA: She has not been sleeping –

AUGUSTINE: What brings us is the love of Jesus Christ!
Listen! One God made all that is! His son
Is Jesus Christ, and he came down from heaven
And lived among us. And the wind obeyed him,
And demons issued at his stern command
Out of the souls of men and women dying
From that inhabitation. At his word
The dead stood up, and walked, and kissed their friends,
He had the power to undo disaster.
And the blind leaders of the blind condemned him,
And hanged him from a crossbeam by his hands
Until the breath of life passed out of him.
But on the third day after that – oh listen! –
The tomb released him! And he rose to heaven,
When he had talked and eaten with his loved ones.
And he will come again to rule a kingdom

Of peace and rightness that will have no end.
I am the herald of the King of Heaven!

OSBERT: Er... the son of a god called God, came to
earth, and then he was hanged on a beam –

ETHELBERT: Yes.

OSBERT: He died.

ETHELBERT: Yes.

OSBERT: But rose again.

ETHELBERT: Ah!

OSBERT: And he will return at some point.

ETHELBERT: Excellent.

TATA: Mother –

BERTHA: God is love! Out of love for you he came down!

ETHELBERT: Well, I'm glad it wasn't out of love for you.

AUGUSTINE: We do not say that your beliefs are evil,
But that they are a sieve through which the spirit
Leaks away slowly to be lost in darkness.
We offer you a golden cup, a chalice
Without a crack, that holds our Lord's forgiveness.

BERTHA: Stupendous! Oh marvellous!

ETHELBERT: What did he say? That was a very
tender note.

OSBERT: He commiserates with our beliefs, King. He
says they are not wicked, but utterly useless and that
we are lost.

BERTHA: He brings you forgiveness!

ETHELBERT: Priestess, what do you think?

PRIESTESS: This god can love me if he likes, but I don't
love him. As for forgiveness, let him forgive his
enemies. I've done nothing to him.

OSBERT: The love –

ETHELBERT: No, Osbert. Augustine. Reply.

AUGUSTINE: You think that God is multiple and cruel,
I tell you he is love and he is one;
The proof is this: he died on earth for you,
And opened heaven to the heart of man.

BERTHA: Praise God!

TATA: She's not well –

ETHELBERT: Come on, Osbert!

BERTHA: The truth needs no interpretation! This man
speaks fire. Let him stay with us! God is with him!

ETHELBERT: I wish God spoke English.

OSBERT: He says that God is very magnificent –

*ETHELBERT stops OSBERT and, after examining
AUGUSTINE, leaves. His court follow.*

AUGUSTINE: The king was moved.

SEVERUS: There should have been a sign.
What was the sign?

AUGUSTINE: The sign was his reaction.

SEVERUS: He should have seen the light immediately –
People will say he came and went away
Slightly confused but otherwise unchanged.
God is not with us!

AUGUSTINE: He is not with you!
Spare me this congregation of the faithless,
Like loose bells tied around my neck that jingle

At every step I take! To come from Rome
Through fire and thunder in the company
Of dust, of dead things! When Christ comes again,
What will you tell him?

LAURENCE: Feed upon your faith,
You starved snake! Heaven thundered through
                                        Augustine!
An angel took his place and spoke through him!

SEVERUS: I can't go on – my skin is quivering –

Enter TATA.

TATA: You may remain! You have convinced the king
That you are not insane. Congratulations!

Exit TATA.

LAURENCE: Now to the capital at Canterbury!
Caesar was slower! Only Christ has power!

SEVERUS: It would be sad to disappoint the princess.

LAURENCE: Forward in God, to claim his victory!

AUGUSTINE: Striving to copy his humility.

Exeunt.

ACT TWO

Scene 1

Near a field of battle on the Welsh border. Enter ST DAVID'S, ELWY, DINOTH and OLWEN. The men of God fling themselves to their knees and raise their arms to heaven.

ELWY: Now brothers, we must fling ourselves at heaven,
    Crying like crows that struggle after eagles,
    Too far, too high, beyond their bodies' powers,
    Here by this field of battle on our border
    Where for our king and Christ our warriors
    Are pressed against the English. Now from Wales,
    Take back the whole of Britain; make this hour
    The everlasting tomb of Ethelfrith.

DINOTH: Oh God, turn back the starving sea that strains
    In rage against us, hungry for our homes,
    And give us back this country, that was once
    Ours from the western to the eastern ocean.

ST DAVID'S: Almighty God! This people is your own!
    When Joseph journeyed from Jerusalem,
    Our priests the druids left their holy stones
    And fell to loving you. But since that time,
    This Christian race has burned in pagan flames!

OLWEN: (*Waking from a trance.*)
    Only a little English fox is torn.

DINOTH: What does she mean? Speak plainly like
                                a Christian!

Enter ANEIRIN.

ANEIRIN: Listen, you echoes of the endless word,
    You men in cowls who call on God to kill.

ST DAVID'S: Aneirin, is the Lord for us or them?

ANEIRIN: I stood on a bright hillside looking to
                                                    the east,
   And at my feet the heather and the grass were tugged
   By the blue infinite of space, and quietness was rife;
   It was the windblown stillness of my country's
                                                    thoughts,
   The song no sword can end. Two walls of shields
                                                    stepped out,
   And with a shout of Jesus one ran to the other
   That like a chalk cliff met the rush and turned it back
   But let a few lumps slip that crashed into the wash,
   Leaving green gaps – I saw the shrieking souls leap up
   Like gulls by sudden updrifts caught and carried off,
   And then the friends behind stepped forward and
                                                    remade
   The wall with their own selves, as April mends the
                                                    world;
   And for a while the air was humming like a lyre
   With arrows and with spears that sped like thrushes,
                                                    flung
   To bury their sharp heads in earth or wood or men,
   Looking for worms where worms would very soon be
                                                    found;
   And the opposing coasts collapsed into the waves,
   And then the rain came down to wash the stained
                                                    swords clean
   That flashed above the press, among the animals
   Head down in scarlet pools; the work of turning men
   To earth was warmly and with good spades carried on;
   But then a rainbow, stretched above the congregation,
   Put heart into the Christians – they began an anthem
   And suddenly the heathens scattered like blown sand.

DINOTH: Praise God!

ANEIRIN: This was the battle of the mud against
                                                    the mud.
   But now the slow crows croak, fold over in the sky,

And float to earth, wings spread and claws stretched
out to grip
Whatever shows above the bog this mad herd churned,
And nature in her many secret processes,
Breaks the remains. The earth makes use of all our wars,
And never stops to stare or holds her breath in awe.

DINOTH: Victory!

OLWEN: No, God looked down and smiled and for
a moment froze
The fate of the defenders, to a later time
Put off the final drowning of the British race.
This is the word of God – King Ethelfrith will come
With vaster armies, quickly, this was just a test
To see if both his hands are needed for our throat.

ST DAVID'S: Well, we have won this day and we will see.
Bishop and abbot, bard and prophetess –
As we have come together to defend
The Christian kingdoms of the land of Wales,
Let us not part, but let us help each other –
At all times praying, listening to heaven.

Exeunt.

Scene 2

ETHELBERT's court. Enter LILLA to ETHELBERT.

LILLA: King, thank you for agreeing to see me!

ETHELBERT: What is your message? They tell me
you have come from Prince Edwin.

LILLA: That hero waits in hiding on your border.
Driven from place to place like a goose, like a wild
duck blown by a tempest –

ETHELBERT: What has happened to this heroic duck? Ethelfrith killed his father, I know, Aelle was a friend of mine.

LILLA: We have passed from kingdom to kingdom. Lately we were in Wales, but now the giant of the north breathes on Wales with his terrible breath and we could not stay –

ETHELBERT: Edwin should know that I would shelter him.

LILLA: He does not wish to bring down on this land the stamping feet of Ethelfrith and his battering hands.

ETHELBERT: I am not afraid of any part of Ethelfrith. Edwin must come to us at once. Fetch him!

LILLA: King! You are a son of Woden! Freya is your wife's mother! Thor is your cousin!

Exit LILLA. Enter OSBERT.

ETHELBERT: Osbert, I don't know what you've got to report today but I can tell you what I want to hear about.

OSBERT: That is exactly what I want to report.

ETHELBERT: Are all my people Christians?

OSBERT: Not yet, King. Estimates differ, but it appears that several thousand have gone over.

ETHELBERT: That's quite a lot to have decided that Christ is their king. Not that I'm jealous. But if everyone was converted except me I'd look a bit silly, wouldn't I? King of myself. And look, Osbert, I have sent for Edwin of Deira, we will shelter him from Ethelfrith. That brings us an inch closer to war. It is the will of Woden. God help us. This is no time for Christ.

OSBERT: Unless Christ is stronger than Woden. But I can't see that he is, nailed hands and feet to a crossbeam! How will he swing his sword, ride his horse, command, do anything?

ETHELBERT: Osbert, they took him down.

OSBERT: Oh I see –

ETHELBERT: These monks are impressive men. Woden must be staring at them fiercer than the sun at a man on a plank in mid-ocean, but they keep their positions – eyes level, shields straight. Now where is my wife, for instance, when I need her?

OSBERT: In the chapel.

ETHELBERT: Ah, that explains the prickling on the back of my neck. Keep praying, darling!

OSBERT: Shall I send for her?

ETHELBERT: You could try, Osbert, or you could try to eat your own head, and see which worked better. Yes, I would like to see her, but if it will be it will be, that's all I can say.

OSBERT: King, I will at least linger outside the chapel.

ETHELBERT: Alright!

Exit OSBERT.

ETHELBERT: Well, my Bertha, you would come if you knew how my heart aches to know what you're thinking! But you're locked up in a bright cave and I'm out in the moon howling. She won't come, she won't come.

Enter TATA.

TATA: Ethelbert!

ETHELBERT: Bertha! Oh my love! Oh it's Tata! Why did you call me Ethelbert? What's happening?

TATA: There are angels all over the place, father, you
　　can't find a dark corner or a shadow anywhere, it's
　　like the town's on fire.

ETHELBERT: There's a lot of chanting going on,
　　I know that.

TATA: We can't ignore it, we can't refuse to be moved, we
　　have to make a stand against it or get caught up in it.

ETHELBERT: You're right.

TATA: Bertha is here.

ETHELBERT: Good.

TATA: She can't stay away anymore, she's on fire with
　　heavenly love.

ETHELBERT: Well, I won't stand against that!

TATA: The monks are all praying that she'll make
　　an impression.

ETHELBERT: I see. It's a plot!

TATA: If it fails she will die.

ETHELBERT: I won't kill her!

TATA: But she will die.

ETHELBERT: You keep saying she's going to die and
　　then, Woden! – the next day she shows up again
　　perfectly healthy.

TATA: Not this time.

ETHELBERT: Really? Well, I suppose anything
　　can happen in these religious festivals.

TATA: What will you do about it? Her life is in
　　your hands.

ETHELBERT: Oh our lives are always in each other's
　　hands. But answer me this, Tata – if she loves me,

why must there be this other one? I know that with you he must be everything. Well, what's left for me?

TATA: You must speak to her. I can't tell you that your wife loves you.

ETHELBERT: What can I say? Send her through to me, Christ help me, Woden go away. If it happens, it happens.

TATA: It's easy to pretend.

ETHELBERT: Out of my sight, daughter of Loki! Kings don't fake.

TATA: I'm gone.

Exit.

ETHELBERT: My daughter is a true child of the old gods, without knowing it.

Enter WODEN, LOKI and FREYA.

Woden, Loki, Freya, old friends. How I love your ways. You are chaos, which is the truth! My mother's mother told my mother, and my mother told me that this world is shifty, and I have seen for myself that she was not lying. All wounds and bone-weariness and the deep deep darkness that sits on my finger day and night, only add to it. You may say that I am a great king, but things have not always gone my way. For example there is this painful love I have for my wife, which is certainly a curse. It won't let me rest. Now my old wicked friends, you see that you have come between us, you and all my ancestors. Love drives you out. Go! Go! But imagine the horror – a perfect God! And what will we do on Wodensday and Thorsday and Freyasday? But without Christ I can't have her. And I can't die of love, I'm too tough.

Exeunt GODS. Enter BERTHA.

BERTHA: My love.

ETHELBERT: Bertha.

BERTHA: Osbert said you wanted to see me.

ETHELBERT: How right he was.

BERTHA: What is it?

EHTHELBERT: The exile Edwin has asked to stay at our court. Of course this would cross Ethelfrith. War. Mayhem. Murder.

BERTHA: I am glad that you wanted to see me.

ETHELBERT: Of course I wanted to see you.

BERTHA: I am sure that you have not refused Prince Edwin.

ETHELBERT: I have not. That was right, was it?

BERTHA: That was a good act. That is what I would expect.

ETHELBERT: I was terrified of Ethelfrith – not for myself but for our people. Now I am not.

BERTHA: That is what I am for.

ETHELBERT: Nothing can shake me when you stand with me like this.

BERTHA: It is the Holy Spirit.

ETHELBERT: While I was waiting, you know, I said goodbye to some friends of mine forever – Woden, Loki, Freya.

BERTHA: Thank God.

ETHELBERT: Now I have nothing but you, Bertha.

BERTHA: Nothing?

ETHELBERT: Nothing.

BERTHA: (*Explodes.*) Oh you are so close!

ETHELBERT: To what?

BERTHA: God has sent you so many signs, in his love
for you he has directed with his own hands these
forty monks to you. Can't you see the world is
coming to an end! Cross over to me!

ETHELBERT: I have come halfway.

BERTHA: Keep going! Keep going! I am not God!
This sign is all you need! Outside of this there is
nothing. If you do not take up Christ's cross you
will never find me!

ETHELBERT: But you came to me.

BERTHA: I am not here. I am in heaven.

ETHELBERT: Come down.

BERTHA: If you will not change then this is how it
will be! Seize me now! I will not come again!

ETHELBERT: I do not know that I can bear
such honesty.

BERTHA: Good because from now on it is
all pretending!

ETHELBERT: Oh Woden take me back!

BERTHA: Woden is for children! I will not be married
to a child! It is all just your mother's stories!

ETHELBERT: Enemy!

BERTHA: I was your wife!

Exit BERTHA and ETHELBERT different ways in tears.

Scene 3

ETHELBERT's palace. Enter LILLA and EDWIN.

EDWIN: We're beggars, Lilla, she won't like us.

LILLA: We're on her trail now. I saw her going this way, my Lord. She was humming.

EDWIN: What does she look like?

LILLA: She's got a beautiful back of the head.

EDWIN: So, Lilla, she's not here. What do I do next?

LILLA: She's coming back! Oh, she's stopped to look out of a window. What people usually do now is hide and then step out at an appropriate moment.

EDWIN: Alright.

He hides.

LILLA: She's still looking out of the window. What can she see? Who's she spying on? A monk adjusting his tights? A queen kissing a tree? These are the kind of things we see out of windows passing by; we'd better be careful, wherever we are – and now there's this god called Jesus who sees inside you; what am I inside? Not Lilla at all. There is a skill we warriors have, to turn into any animal we want at any time and so escape. I am a sheep at home in the mountains. A simple beast, but a fierce believer in Woden, so keep out, Jesus, respect my curtains. I need that place! Baaa! In a thick fleece of fog I lay me down to sleep. Keep away, good shepherd! I hope you never find me. Ah! Is she stirring? No. The queen's climbed into the tree, and the monk sits down underneath it and takes out his make-up. In our wanderings we have learnt to cotton on quick to the situation. Here the king serves Woden and the

queen is a Christian and there's this princess in
between I think my Lord should be interested in.
She's coming! The sight of me would stop her
singing, but I vanish back to the mountains of Deira.
(*He leaves slowly on all fours. TATA enters and walks past him,
not seeing him as he exits.*)

TATA: (*Sings to a lyre.*)
Now Heimdal blows his golden horn,
Trumpeting that the end has come,
There will not be another dawn,
Time has brought round the hour of doom.

The dead souls shake along hell's road
And to the sky the waters climb,
Yggdrasil bends beneath that load,
Doom has brought round the end of time.

With happiness the ravens sing,
The wolf is feasting in the hall,
Woden drank wisdom from the spring,
But he too must descend to hell.

Hrym from the east rides, shield upraised,
And the world-serpent writhes and thrashes,
Men fall whose deeds will not be praised,
To the dark earth the bright sky crashes –

EDWIN appears halfway through this. He applauds.

TATA: I thought I was alone.

EDWIN: I have no trumpets
Walking before me, all the noise I make
Is the soft rustle of my shadow dragging
Over the flagstones.

TATA: Did you like my song?

EDWIN: It was surprising. Yes, I do like songs.

TATA: Who taught you Latin?

EDWIN: In my wanderings
   I have been forced to study languages
   More difficult than Latin.

TATA: When I ask you
   A direct question, why do you reply
   To your own question which you did not say?

EDWIN: You must be Princess Tata. I have heard
   That you are fierce. If we are to collide,
   Shall we speak English?

TATA: In your wanderings
   You have picked up the knack of saying nothing,
   But I have learnt the trick of repetition
   By staying put. And so I ask again,
   Who taught you Latin?

EDWIN: When I started out,
   I had a retinue of fighting men,
   The sons of executed noblemen,
   Exiled with me. Wherever I appeared,
   Nobody ever asked me who I was,
   My title and my name and history
   Preceded my approach like weather-signs,
   Thunderbugs, fir-cones opening and so on.

TATA: Who taught you Latin?

EDWIN: So as time went on –

TATA: You are Prince Edwin of Northumbria.

EDWIN: No, of Deira.

TATA: Now Northumbria.
   And you were exiled by King Ethelfrith.
   Well, I am not the slightest bit surprised.
   You are the most infuriating person
   That I have ever spoken to. If I
   Was Ethelfrith, I would have exiled you
   To a small rock off Scotland, gagged and bound,

To listen to the questions of the tide
And answer indirectly till you drowned.
Who taught you Latin?

EDWIN: Now as I was saying –
My company of friends disintegrated –
All but one faithful man – where is he now –
Some killed in fair fight, others lured away
To kill for some wild Irish king for pay –
Some drowned in bogs, some married, some waylaid;
And as I wandered, never staying long,
To Scotland and to Ireland and to Wales,
I was disturbed to find myself, at last,
Having to answer for myself – however,
What is my answer? I am from Deira,
A country that does not exist –

TATA: Now listen,
I have a question, and I have a reason
For asking it – whoever taught you Latin,
Was he a Christian, and are you a Christian?

EDWIN: Well, I must answer if there is a reason!

TATA: A question is a reason for an answer!

EDWIN: It is. Forgive me, but good friends of mine
Have answered questions that were put for reasons,
And they are in the ground. By hesitation
I have survived so far all such inquiries.

TATA: I see –

EDWIN: A question from a strong position
Is like an arrow falling from a castle –

TATA: Best not to face it.

EDWIN: But the questioner
Is you, and so I stand my ground, and gladly
Wait to be wounded. I am not a Christian.

TATA: Then I am safe from being blamed for singing
    The songs I like.

EDWIN: Is this the situation?

TATA: My mother loves my father terribly;
    That is a secret that she keeps from him,
    Because she is a Christian. Do you see –
    He is a pagan, and she wants to change him,
    To keep him with her when their hearts stop beating.
    Who taught you Latin?

EDWIN: I was taught by Britons
    In Wales, and they are Christians, but their customs
    Forbid them to convert an Englishman.

TATA: The Romans are the opposite!

EDWIN: But Woden
    Is sure enough that we will not desert him.

TATA: We? Who are we?

EDWIN: Princess, I beg your pardon.
    I understood that you are not a Christian.

TATA: Not Christian, but I am no friend of Woden.

EDWIN: Who do you worship then?

TATA: Myself or no-one.

EDWIN: It is the doctrine of a kingless person.
    Myself or no-one will be useful to you
    If you are ever exiled.

TATA: But you said
    That you serve Woden.

EDWIN: Did I? Did I really?

TATA: Poor Edwin, autumn leaf, do you agree
    With everyone, no matter what they say?

EDWIN: Not with myself. No matter what I say.

TATA: Why not?

EDWIN: Because, unlike your new religion,
      I am too easy to disprove.

TATA: My friend,
      Why do you call my feelings a religion?
      It is because I follow no religion
      That I have felt them. And I came to them
      Only for this: to rip up all religions
      And stuff them in a box and step on them.

EDWIN: And I believe in that.

TATA: Believe in nothing!

EDWIN: Alright! I will if you insist – your vision
      Is so convincing.

TATA: It is not a vision!
      And I am not its prophet or its bishop,
      It is just nothing. Do you understand?

EDWIN: Yes, with some effort I can understand
      Nothing.

TATA: I have a space inside my mind,
      Not for a god, but for a human being
      Whom I will love, and who will love me only,
      Not slipping half his heart into the sky
      Behind my back –

EDWIN: And you and he will pray
      To one another, vanish when you die
      Into each other for eternity.

      EDWIN sees BERTHA coming. TATA exits in confusion.

      *Enter BERTHA, AUGUSTINE, LAURENCE, SEVERUS
      and ALBANUS.*

AUGUSTINE: The edges of this island
   Are still inhabited by men called Britons,
   Christians, but darkened by new customs grown
   In separation since the legions left them.
   We must invite them back into Christ's empire.
   King Ethelfrith is threatening their kingdoms
   With swift extinction – if King Ethelbert
   Of Kent would only join our faith, and after,
   Reach out in friendship to the British Christians,
   To make a league of peace against the heathens!

EDWIN: They hate the English more than death itself,
   Because this island was their own land once.

AUGUSTINE: But will they hate the Christian English?

EDWIN: Yes:
   They would not even speak about religion
   To me when I was with them – and to them
   I was a decent kind of Englishman.

AUGUSTINE: Then we must climb their hills of pride
                              and heal them.
   Christ is already founded in this country,
   In darkness all around us – we have only
   To light a candle in this cave to see
   Jewels in the ceiling.

LAURENCE: When Augustine speaks,
   Not even stones could fail to hear Christ through him!

Enter ETHELBERT, wrapped in a blanket, and OSBERT.

BERTHA: So you will meet our British friends.
                       And listen:
   I want to send a representative
   Of our house to the west with you, Augustine.
   Who can we send except my daughter Tata?

ETHELBERT: What is this discussion? Are you taking
   over my kingdom, Augustine? What is it to do with

Edwin? Why do you mention the British? These are dangerous things to be saying! Explain yourselves to the king!

BERTHA: Your Majesty, we are simply discussing the idea of a mission to the Christians in Wales, with perhaps Edwin and Tata accompanying, to suggest to those godly people, threatened by Ethelfrith, that they might join with us in faith –

ETHELBERT: The British? Witches! Break up this meeting! I will not have my queen discussing politics with foreigners while I, the king, must stand listening like a horse! Woden! You have pushed me too far! You have gone too fast, Augustine! I could send you headless back to Rome today! Send Tata and Edwin to Wales? Edwin? Who is he? Nowhere, son of nothing! Madness! Get out, get out, all of you! Oh!

He collapses.

BERTHA: What is it? My God, I have done this.

ETHELBERT: Just the death of Ethelbert the Sweet. You've killed the donkey and set a lion on the throne! I am alright, I am alright.

ETHELBERT shoos them all out and is himself helped off by OSBERT. Re-enter AUGUSTINE, as if to follow ETHELBERT and plead with him, but then stopping.

AUGUSTINE: King! King! But he will not turn back
                                                    for me;
The pride in him disdains the pride in me.
How can I change him? I am steeped in sin –
Ten thousand lost souls gathered by my mission,
Christ is in my hand, that healed the lame and blind,
And a queen heaping praises on my name.
Oh there are jagged shards of self in me –
I am the child that clambered over tombs

Of Caesars, mocked their broken columns,
All history a heap of marble debris
Compared to what I knew. And I constructed
From Christ, the pride of twenty emperors!
That I must now tear down and turn to ruins.

Re-enter ETHELBERT.

ETHELBERT: Ah, Augustine, forgive me for my fury.
   I went out full of Woden, but halfway through the
   door, found myself empty. Birdsong blew me back in.

AUGUSTINE: O King, I cannot understand your
                       language,
   But I can see that you are full of trouble.
   I think we should confess to one another,
   Speak from the heart, since we are free of meaning.

ETHELBERT: Not understanding is the root of all my
   fury. I am sure the sea wrecks ships just because it
   cannot grasp them.

AUGUSTINE: All things exist beyond the human mind;
   Almost at times it seems that we are worms
   Eating a mountain of incomprehension.

ETHELBERT: Three small things are beyond me –
   God, my wife, and what on earth you are saying.

AUGUSTINE: You are a king. But you have shrugged
                       off pride
   To speak to me, and let your sorrow show;
   Pride is a plain of ice on which I glide
   Helplessly from horizon to horizon.

ETHELBERT: What a sad pair of men! Like the last
   survivors of two opposing armies, who come together
   among the corpses, wondering, shall we fight, shall
   we weep? God help me, monk, I have set her up in
   heaven, from which I have torn down everything else!
   I would gladly let in a little divinity to our despair.
   I have exhausted my incomprehension, and I am left

with no plan of my own. I must be humbled, limp
back from my strong position, admit that my high
ground is not worth defending. Oh heaven, make me
sweet, and make her to listen!

AUGUSTINE: Although you are a king you come
                                    before me
In this affair of falling down. Forgive me!
God! God!

ETHELBERT: Bertha! Bertha!

AUGUSTINE: And she is coming. As she hurries in,
One day my God, the king of light, will come.

Exit AUGUSTINE. Enter BERTHA.

BERTHA: King? Husband?

ETHELBERT: Wife?

BERTHA: How are you?

ETHELBERT: Oh my love, I believe –

BERTHA: Believe what?

ETHELBERT: I believe that we are alone.

BERTHA: That's good.

ETHELBERT: What did you come to say to me?

BERTHA: Nothing.

ETHELBERT: But it's years since you've stood with
me like this.

BERTHA: What a shame.

ETHELBERT: What has happened?

BERTHA: You fell down. I could not go on.

ETHELBERT: Have you been praying for me?

BERTHA: An answer came: stop trying to convert him.

ETHELBERT: But I want to be converted!

BERTHA: Oh.

ETHELBERT: I want you to teach me.

BERTHA: Never mind that.

ETHELBERT: I think I could believe.

BERTHA: Oh be quiet!

ETHELBERT: I do believe! Nothing separates us!

BERTHA: Then be quiet!

ETHELBERT: I can't be quiet! Call the monks, give me a sermon!

BERTHA: Oh bugger the monks!

ETHELBERT: Call them immediately!

BERTHA: Tomorrow, tomorrow.

ETHELBERT: Tomorrow.

Exeunt.

ACT THREE

Scene 1

Wales. Enter ELWY, DINOTH, ANEIRIN, OLWEN.

OLWEN: It is because the Romans have returned!

DINOTH: The Romans?

ELWY: With their legions? Dead and gone!

OLWEN: There is a lion in the cage of Rome.

ELWY: What does this mean?

OLWEN: The echo of his roar
    Will seek you out. You will receive a letter
    And that will be a gap in doom, a chasm
    For you to slip through quick; but in return
    You must drink bitter water that will force you
    To vomit up the feast of pride that fills you.

DINOTH: And that will save us from King Ethelfrith?

ELWY: If we serve Rome –

ANEIRIN: Expect a letter soon.

ELWY: Nothing might happen. God may disobey
    The prophecies of this half-Christian woman!

Enter ST DAVID'S with a letter.

ST DAVID'S: Praise God!

ELWY: For what?

ST DAVID'S: A letter from the Romans.

ELWY: What does it say?

ST DAVID'S: It speaks of an alliance
    Between our kingdoms and the Christian English
    Of Kent, against King Ethelfrith.

DINOTH: (*Tempted.*)   God help us –

ELWY: The Christian English! And perhaps the devil
    Is Christian too, and ripe for an alliance!

DINOTH: What does this swordless emperor demand?

ELWY: Our calculation of the date of Easter
    Is wrong, he says, and we must change our method.

DINOTH: What else?

ELWY: Our tonsure is not right by him.

ST DAVID'S: So shave our heads! But that is all,
                                        companions!

ELWY: No, no, he saves the worst till last. He wants us
    To preach the life of Jesus to the English –

DINOTH: To our invaders?

ELWY: Can this man not see
    That we are standing on the last green hill
    Waiting for Christ to carry us away?
    We will not do it!

OLWEN: Listen to the wind!
    The oak, the holly and the ash are singing
    About your last breath. Everything is turning,
    The eagle wheeling to the place appointed
    For your destruction, the worm journeying
    Through the dark ground to where you will be lying,
    The stars all stepping quickly to the station
    That marks your end. And yet the wheel delays,
    Slowed by the hand of God, and there is time
    For the destruction of the British people
    To change, enchanted into God knows what
    Miracle of forgiveness. Men of God,
    Fast, and rise early, fling yourselves unclothed
    On the sharp stars preceding dawn, be humble,
    And even now your Father will forgive you,
    Keep off the deathday that is waiting for you.

ANEIRIN: There is an oak tree in the border country,
　　That was beloved when our forefathers
　　Followed the druids – foreigners possess
　　The land around it, but the ground beneath it
　　Is British to the centre of the earth,

ELWY: This is the place where we must meet Augustine!

　　Exeunt.

Scene 2

ETHELBERT's court.

ETHELBERT: Shall I speak Latin?

AUGUSTINE:　　　　　　　　If you wish to, King.
　　My master in this letter recommends
　　His friend Paulinus to Your Majesty.

ETHELBERT: You are most welcome to our court,
　　　　　　　　　　　　　　Paulinus.

PAULINUS: I have heard much about the thunderstorm
　　Of baptisms that has embraced your kingdom.
　　Seventy thousand in one afternoon.

AUGUSTINE: Only ten thousand.

PAULINUS:　　　　　　　Is that all? Forgive me.

ETHELBERT: Speak to the Welsh for Rome and for
　　　　　　　　　　　　　　our kingdom,
　　Offering love. And I have asked Prince Edwin
　　To be your guide. He knows them well.
　　God shield you.

BERTHA: Augustine, God is sitting on your shoulder,
　　If you can spread throughout this fighting island
　　The light you have set up in one small corner,
　　You will have saved four peoples from destruction.

ETHELBERT staggers.

BERTHA: What is it?

ETHELBERT: Just a sliding in my veins;
    Feeding on God, the heart has grown too strong
    For all the other organs, and they strain
    Like shouting stones. God lifts me like a pawn
    And sets me down a little further on.
    I am alright, don't fuss, I am alright.
    Send Tata to the west to meet the British.
    Rancour will vanish when they see my Tata.

Exeunt.

Scene 3

A forest on the way from Kent to the Wessex border. Enter SEVERUS.

SEVERUS: I am the oak and the pine, everything that
    dies is mine. These are my woods! Stop! Saint
    Bridget! Wandering light, slow down. Where are you
    taking me, darting about? Little wren, little wren,
    wait! Oh don't turn into the boar with horns, oh
    don't let the wolf stand up. Oh Jesus! Virgin!

Enter LILLA running.

LILLA: Woden! Woden! Oh there you are! I've found
    you! All your friends are looking for you – but I'm
    your only real friend. Tell me things!

SEVERUS: I am the boar! Look out!

*He grunts and charges LILLA, winding him. He runs out,
leaving LILLA writhing, who then gets up.*

LILLA: We have been walking for three weeks through
    this wood. That's not what you'd call a stroll through
    the trees. At first it is, but then it becomes a series
    of strolls, with nothing between them, so that they

become not strolls at all, but something extremely
serious. A tree on its own is one thing, but when they
get together in a gang and whisper – or when you get
right inside and there's no wind – I have never suffered
such composure. The monks can't take it! This is
a sacred place. Which makes it even more difficult for
me to break my conscience. I want Edwin to be with
this woman alone, but it's impossible, because I am
always there! If I would only accidentally stroll over
a cliff! But there are no cliffs here. Or if I could stray
foolishly and lose myself and pine away. That ought to
be easy. Perhaps I am lost now. Yes, I have done it!
Victory! I am Lilla no longer, just a question of
waiting till the breathing finishes.

Enter EDWIN and TATA.

EDWIN: Lilla!

LILLA: Oh you fools, pretend you haven't seen, stroll on!

TATA: Why? We came to find you!

LILLA: Don't you ever want to be alone?

TATA: Not yet.

LILLA: Well, you never will, you never will, you
never will!

TATA: Why?

LILLA: Don't you understand that only by my death
can you ever find happiness?

TATA: I think we got here just in time.

EDWIN: Lilla, you mustn't wander off on your own,
you get too excited.

AUGUSTINE: (*Off.*) Severus!

EDWIN: Here come the monks.

LILLA: I'm a great fire in the dark, everyone gathers to me.

Enter SEVERUS running, followed by LAURENCE, AUGUSTINE, ALBANUS and PAULINUS. They surround him.

AUGUSTINE: Severus, brother!

SEVERUS: These are my woods. What are you doing here, men of God, your Christ is in a dry place, no trees there, nothing but sticks in the wind.

AUGUSTINE: In the name of Christ, I command you, Woden, out of him!

LILLA: This man is blessed! Tell us more, friend! Gather round – Woden, Woden!

AUGUSTINE: Out, out, by the blood of Christ!

LILLA: People walk into the forest for weeks, fast, cut themselves, sit up all night naked in the frost to get to this state – don't spoil it –

LAURENCE: We don't want it, Englishman. We have not journeyed all this way from Rome to become worshippers of Woden! By the blood of Christ!

LILLA: You Christians are so stingy! Why one God? Am I one person?

AUGUSTINE: We must cast out this devil with strong prayers!

ALBANUS: You must begin them. We are just like him, Blinded by Woden!

AUGUSTINE: Everyone kneel down.

All kneel with eyes closed except LILLA.

God clear these woods that crowd into the mind,
Trapping us in this twilight of the spirit,

Blue mornings, orange afternoons, green evenings,
And then the branch-roofed night that groans with
                                                    omens,
Screened from the vast intelligence of heaven.

SEVERUS: We will rip the man when we find him, we
will nail the rag of his heart to the cross of the
world, we will wolf him!

AUGUSTINE: God sacrifice this darkness to yourself,
Unchain our treebound brother Severus
Who walks with elves and talks with oaks and spirits –

SEVERUS: Sit down, Christ! Sit down and eat with
Woden! Thor, come, with fire, roast Augustine! Let
all the company of gods sit down, let Hel drag up
a bench –

AUGUSTINE: And let the only wood we look upon
Be the six pieces stripped of everything
But dying men, outside Jerusalem.

SEVERUS: Feast on the long-limbed king, fruit of our
hunting! Come Freya, cut him, hand round the red
wine! Freya! Woden!

*TATA sings. Everyone goes into a state of prayer except
EDWIN. She addresses the song to him.*

TATA: Love my heaven in a cloud,
Stepping heavy on the ground,
Tell me will you come to me
When the night is old and angry?

Love my heaven in the sun,
Sleeping bloodless underground
Tell me will you come to me
When the day is young and sorry?

Love my heaven in the rain,
Stooping, touching, making well,
Tell me will you come to me
When the morning steps up sharply?

Love my heaven in the end,
When the sun is up completely,
Tell me you will come to me,
Tell me how I will be happy.

SEVERUS falls asleep.

LAURENCE: Thank God!

AUGUSTINE: Carry him back to where the men
are waiting.

Exeunt. Re-enter LILLA and TATA.

LILLA: No, don't follow me!

TATA: Why not?

LILLA: Slip away when I'm blinking! Evade me!

TATA: Why, Lilla?

LILLA: Don't you understand about Edwin? He's not
a fixture, like your father, he's a scarecrow's coat,
fate blows on him, he'll fall apart, he'll disappear
downwind with a panicky flapping. Ah! Ah! I can't
stand it!

TATA: What's the matter, Lilla? You won't ever be
parted from him.

LILLA: But you will! Listen – now, hear my confession
– your mother made me promise something.

TATA: What?

LILLA: That I would not let you and Edwin have each
other in some wayside barn.

TATA: Oh! Good!

LILLA: But it was the wrong promise! He's my Lord!
I beg you Tata, tie me up – run rings around me,
trick me, or if you're feeling unimaginative, hit
me over the head. Look, I'm looking in the other
direction, creep up behind me.

TATA: Do you really want me to?

LILLA: Hit hard!

TATA: (*She creeps up and strokes the back of his head.*) I can't do it.

LILLA: Ah you poor beautiful fools! Don't you
understand that after this journey you will never see
him again? It will all be people like me.

TATA: I try to understand, but I just can't see it.

LILLA: I have told Prince Edwin what I know to be
true, that after we return from this mission it will be
time for him to move on. I know when Ethelfrith is
getting close, I can always sense it.

TATA: I'm sure you can.

Enter EDWIN.

LILLA: Oh! Queen Bertha, try to understand, the
warrior code eclipses your wishes. I have struggled,
Edwin, my Lord, and your cause has won. I leave
you now, alone for the first and last time, with
your lady.

Exit.

EDWIN: Lilla!

LILLA: (*Off.*) No, my Lord!

TATA: He says that we are in a tragedy.
Why are we failing to despair, my friend?
There is no hope for us that I can see.

EDWIN: We must have eaten something stupefying.

TATA: How can there be a sense of tragedy
Where there are no horizons? Obviously
Distance is necessary to despair,
And at close quarters no-one is unhappy.

EDWIN: What are our options?

TATA: They are all curtailed.

EDWIN: We could escape.

TATA: You need my father's help.
 Who else will help you if you run away,
 Stealing the daughter of your host?

EDWIN: I know.

TATA: It looks as though we ought to be in tears.
 This is our only moment, and the monks are tearing
 Through the trees towards us, knees high.

EDWIN: Should we be dead?

TATA: Or in each other's arms,
 Naked inside some shaken holly bower?

EDWIN: The stars for that are drifting out of line.

TATA: The moon is losing contact with the sea.

EDWIN: So we will never have embraced each other.

TATA: It is the most outrageous prophecy
 That ever happened to an unbeliever,
 That I am not in any kind of hurry,
 No need to pray, or kill myself, or scream;
 It is a bit like Christ as they describe him,
 Except that this creeps up unforced like mushrooms;
 I could reach out and touch my certainty,
 Out of the darkness comes this prophecy,
 That you will not be torn away from me.

EDWIN: I will be thrown into the world again
 And passed like some old joke from hand to hand.
 But this has happened, and will not be changed,
 And for all time this moment is my home.

Enter LILLA, walking backwards with his hands over his eyes.

LILLA: Monks! Monks! Monks!

Enter SEVERUS, AUGUSTINE, LAURENCE, PAULINUS.

SEVERUS: Forgive me, friends! The moon was in my
mind!

PAULINUS: It was your song that saved him from the
demon!

AUGUSTINE: Now quickly to the oak, Christ clear
the road.

LAURENCE: Surely this healing has convinced you,
Edwin?

EDWIN: Love is my God.

LAURENCE: Then you are almost Christian!

Exeunt.

Scene 4

At the cave of the hermit Colman in Wales. Enter ABBOT DINOTH, ST DAVID'S, ELWY, ANEIRIN and OLWEN.

ST DAVID'S: Companions, can we with an open mind
Approach the refuge of this saint as one?

ELWY: How can the offspring of barbarians,
Barbarians themselves, do anything
But get drunk on the blood of God, the wine
That turns to Christ on a believer's tongue,
But to the damned is pure intoxication?

DINOTH: This man Augustine has fed pearls to swine,
And they will turn and rend him in the end.

ST DAVID'S: We who are wineskins of the blood
of Jesus
Must always strive for peace and heal old wounds.

We need the wisdom of the holy man
Whose cave this is, to ask him if Augustine
Is to be trusted as a man of God.
Do we agree?

DINOTH: When Colman speaks, I listen.
Colman is mighty! He has lived alone
For thirty years –

OLWEN: The cave in which he prays
Goes right into the centre of the mountain;
There at the bottom of a lake of darkness
He drinks the silence, listening to heaven.
Around him seams of coal and copper dream,
And the sidhe flock to dance upon his heartbeat,
This man who in the belly of the dragon,
The darkest place in God's creation, shines.

DINOTH: Although he will have heard our prayers, he
rarely
Comes to the surface. When he does, the trees
Bow, and the squirrels bring him nuts and barley.
We will be lucky if he comes.

ELWY: I see him!

ST DAVID'S: Colman!

Enter COLMAN. They all fall to their knees.

COLMAN: What do you want?

ST DAVID'S: We want to ask a question.

COLMAN: Go on.

ST DAVID'S: There is a Roman called Augustine;
He tells us in a letter that our customs
Diverge from his, and from the ways of Rome.
Now he has called us to a meeting. Colman,
Shall we reject him or shall we obey him
And change our ways?

COLMAN: Obey him if he stands.

Exit COLMAN.

ELWY: What did he mean by that?

DINOTH: A Delphic answer,
Difficult to interpret.

ST DAVID'S: No, I see it –

DINOTH: Obey him if he stands –

ELWY: Or if he flies –
I will obey him if he flies, believe me.
But standing – standing – anyone can stand.

DINOTH: Did he say stand? Or was it understand?
I will obey him if he understands.

ANEIRIN: Obey him if he stands.

OLWEN: The man Augustine
Will be in high state, seated on a throne
Under the oak tree's kingly canopy,
When we arrive – and this will be the sign:
If he stands up to greet you, then obey him,
Because he is a man of God; if not –
Then he will always scorn us and despise us,
And be a Roman emperor towards us –

GEOFF: Ah Colman! Heavenly receptacle!

ELWY: Colman has given us a simple sign,
A test! Augustine must betray himself,
And so release us from all obligations!

ANEIRIN: Or he may stand.

DINOTH: We will be watching him;
And if he keeps his seat we contradict him,
Refuse to be his slaves, make no concessions!

ELWY: Oh he will sit, and we are saved by Colman,
    And by the holy silence of the mountain!

ST DAVID'S: Or he may stand, and then –

    Exeunt.

Scene 5

Enter TATA, AUGUSTINE, LAURENCE, SEVERUS and PAULINUS to the oak tree, PAULINUS and SEVERUS carrying a throne which they set down. AUGUSTINE addresses them.

AUGUSTINE: Brothers, the border with the Welsh
                                    is there,
    Across the river; we will meet them here,
    Under the oak. Be strong, submit to heaven,
    Thank God for our deliverance from Woden.

They all pray separately, except for LAURENCE who hovers near AUGUSTINE.

AUGUSTINE: Now Christ in whom there is no near or
                                         far,
    And Gregory who sent me, be with me,
    Here at the furthest limit of the west
    To which we have yet stretched our faith. From here,
    The hills continue into mystery.
    The eagle sees it, but his mind is strange;
    The buzzard, but his eyes are not like ours.
    Here at another edge of what we know,
    We stick like pins that ignorantly shine
    In a green cushion flung down anywhere.
    Oh keep us close to our home reason here,
    Where our stretched tether seems about to –

LAURENCE: Listen,
    Augustine, there are oaks in Italy;
    Imagine that we are in Italy,

Not far from Rome and holy Gregory,
Where he has sent us for the afternoon
To chew the wad of certain points of doctrine
With some Byzantines – easeful occupation,
Accompanied by raisins and sweet wine,
And the soft comments of a woodpigeon.
You are the only person who can doubt you.

AUGUSTINE: It is our ignorance that troubles me.

LAURENCE: What did we know about the Kentish pagans
    Before we sowed the word of God among them?

AUGUSTINE: I think the Britons are more complicated,
    Already sown and left to grow untended.

LAURENCE: They are a people swaddled thick with pride,
    Living in huts on memories of empire,
    We will be Caesars in their eyes, Augustine.

AUGUSTINE: If it is God's will.

LAURENCE: Now your heart is stirring.

SEVERUS: Augustine, how are we to be to them,
    If we are to fulfil their expectations?

LAURENCE sets up a throne for AUGUSTINE to sit on.

LAURENCE: Of Rome? Not humble, as we met the
                              pagans.
    They will be disappointed if we grovel.
    Imagine how their dark imaginations
    Are blazing with the picture of a Roman –
    Augustine, like Augustus, conqueror
    Of Cleopatra, father of the empire!

PAULINUS: Would Christ have met them sitting on
                              a throne?
    How did that man enter Jerusalem?
    On a white horse with purple banners flying?

SEVERUS: He rode a donkey's colt that stepped on palms.

PAULINUS: Why should the pauper friends of Christ
love kings?

LAURENCE: We shall judge angels, the apostle said,
And that requires a certain gravity.

SEVERUS: Here come the Britons!

*Enter the BRITISH BISHOPS, chanting. They bow to
AUGUSTINE. He does not rise, but simply nods his head
and raises his hand. They turn to one another and nod
vigorously, then sit down on the ground, cross-legged and with
their arms crossed.*

AUGUSTINE: Children of heaven! Far-flung scatterings
Of the bright sower of Jerusalem –

ELWY: Good that you tie us to Jerusalem
And not to Rome.

AUGUSTINE: Why not to Rome?

DINOTH: The Church began in Britain
Before the truth was ever brought to Rome.
Joseph of Arimathaea brought it here
To Glastonbury, and with him, in a bag,
The Holy Grail, from which the Lord drank wine
At the Last Supper.

AUGUSTINE: Jesus gave the keys
Of heaven to St Peter, and he told him,
You are the rock on which my Church is founded –
St Peter was the first bishop of Rome –

DINOTH: No he was not! He never was a bishop!

ELWY: That is a dragon's daydream, smoke and poison!

AUGUSTINE: I come to you in gentleness from Rome
To fetch you back into your mother's arms –

DINOTH: When did we leave them?

AUGUSTINE: When you changed old customs
    For new inventions, wrapped the light of heaven
    In British mist.

ELWY: We drink the blood of Christ
    Out of the cup from which St Peter drank.

AUGUSTINE: Where is this cup?

DINOTH: It is invisible,
    Due to a spell.

ELWY: But when we drink the wine,
    We feel the grail replacing what we handle –

DINOTH: Jerusalem is in the land of Britain!

AUGUSTINE: And shall our centre then be everywhere?
    Wherever men of God feel most at home?
    I say, the new Jerusalem is Rome,
    Accepted by all churches but your own.

DINOTH: Is Rome accepted by Byzantium?

AUGUSTINE: An empire of the spirit has been founded
    At the old centre. Holy Gregory,
    The ruler of the Church –

ELWY: Of yours, not ours!

AUGUSTINE: Brothers in Jesus, can we start again?
    Is it my letter that has hurt you, brothers?
    All I attempted in that document
    Was to put forward subjects for discussion –

ST DAVID'S: And we have come here to discuss them
                                with you,
    As Christ would wish – is that not so, my brothers?

ELWAY: Brother, your letter cut us to the bone.

AUGUSTINE: How can that be?

DINOTH: The question of our tonsure;
   You say that we should shave our heads like yours,
   And sign ourselves the slaves of Rome forever,
   Vow celibacy, change the date of Easter –

ST DAVID'S: These are all subjects we can speak about,
   Although today there is a gulf between us.

AUGUSTINE: And brothers, if we disagree today,
   Praise God! A cause for us to meet again!

DINOTH: But your demand that we should teach
                             the heathen –

AUGUSTINE: That is the simple duty of a Christian.

ST DAVID'S: The sons of the abyss have stained
                             our mind
   With blood no words can ever wash away.
   If we were ever to preach Christ to them,
   What could we say but, sinners, you must go,
   You hold this land against the will of heaven.

AUGUSTINE: All men on earth, no matter what
                            their crimes,
   Are children of the living God – he made them,
   And he forgave them when they crucified him.
   Can we, no matter how they make us suffer,
   Dare to refuse them what our master gave them?

ELWY: They would not stop to listen to our wisdom,
   They would just tear our tongues out.

AUGUSTINE: Gregory,
   The servant of the servants of the Lord –

DINOTH: Tells us to preach to demons – he is wrong.

AUGUSTINE: The voice of Christ on earth has sent
                             me here –

DINOTH: The man you serve is strange and far away,
   He dreams in Rome, while here among the damned
   We fight against the dirt and things are different!

AUGUSTINE: Do you despise the centre of the empire
   You once belonged to?

DINOTH: That was long ago.
   We owe no tribute to the past, Augustine.

AUGUSTINE: Would Christ have left these pagans
                              to damnation?
   He would have healed them; you must teach them.

ELWY: Spirit
   Of desolation! Shall we tell our flock,
   Wolf-harried, that we have misguided them
   For all these years, and led them into error,
   While all around us paces the destroyer?

ST DAVID'S: Brother –

ELWY: This Roman is the devil's rain
   That rots God's weapons!

AUGUSTINE: Is that what I am?
   Brothers, I am incredibly surprised –

ELWY: It will sink in.

AUGUSTINE: But we must speak like Christians –

ELWY: Row Anglesey across the sea, fling Snowdon
   Into the steaming vat of the Atlantic,
   But you will never alter our religion.
   You heathens' friend, you shadow of a Caesar,
   Worm in the carcass of the Roman Empire!

AUGUSTINE: Dear Christ!

DINOTH: You curse us?

AUGUSTINE: You are dead to heaven!
   And your religion is a dark invention –

Spun from the bones of sacrificial children –
It is the purple cloak in which the soldiers
Dressed Christ to mock him when they spat on him.
I tell you this, if you refuse our love,
Hatred will drag you to the pit of hell!
If you refuse to teach these pagans peace,
Then at the swordpoint they will teach you war,
And there will be no sequel to that lesson,
You will be wiped out. Still you people cling
Like seaweed to the edges of the land,
But you are weak, and you will not grow stronger –
Unite with us, and with the Christian English,
Two nations with one faith against the darkness.
Let all the peoples in this land of patches
Be one in faith, or else the weak will perish!

OLWEN: We want to vanish back into the ground.
We were once mountains, and will be again.

DINOTH: We came. Your scorn has driven us away.

ST DAVID'S: God heals all things, and this will mend
in time.

PAULINUS: But time will end! Forgiveness must
come soon!
Friends, we are tables laden with Christ's goodness,
We should sit down and feast on one another,
Leave words to tumble in the grass like puppies
While we sit brothered with the stars in silence.

ST DAVID'S: Friend, we have spoken, and will eat
our words
If God speaks out for Rome and for Augustine.

AUGUSTINE: Tata, we are confounded, speak for us!

*Enter a PEASANT WOMAN, a refugee, with EDWIN and
LILLA.*

WOMAN: Whoever you are, you must leave this place!
They have burnt our village. Let me go!

EDWIN: Tell us who they are.

WOMAN: Ethelfrith's men! They have crossed the
    border! Everyone is running! Whoever they capture
    they torture!

Exit WOMAN.

EDWIN: They are looking for me – and for you, Britons.

LAURENCE: Already God responds to your refusal.

ELWY: This is God's judgement on our souls for leaving
    Our flocks and cells to listen to Augustine!
    Now we must face King Ethelfrith and die.
    He will stand up to greet us certainly.

Exeunt BRITISH.

EDWIN: Tata, go with Augustine and your father's
    soldiers away from the border. I have brought this
    on you. Lilla and I will face these invaders.

LILLA: See, I told you! Today we die! Never hesitate!

EDWIN: We will not fight them.

LILLA: What will we do to them?

EDWIN: Lead them away from Tata.

LILLA: Aha, be foxes!

AUGUSTINE collapses.

LAURENCE: Augustine has been struck down!

SEVERUS: Help him then!

AUGUSTINE: This is my death. To come from Italy
    Only to cause confusion and division,
    And all the struggle of my earthly journey
    Was for destruction – we have lost the Britons.

LAURENCE: The devil sent them – how could we agree
    With hell's battalions?

AUGUSTINE: Quickly back to Kent.
    Laurence, I thank you, you built up my pride
    Into a tower taller than the sky,
    That touched the floor of heaven. It has fallen
    So far that it will never rise again.
    I was too fragile to unite this island,
    It is a great rock lying on my spirit.
    To sleep between these prophecying seas
    Is to wake up deranged by what might be,
    A whirling vane pointing at everything.
    Who'll bind these staves that take such pride
                         in rotting?
    Oh take me quickly back to Canterbury!

He is carried off. Exeunt all but TATA, EDWIN and LILLA.

EDWIN: So we must part, your prophecy was wrong.

TATA: It was the truth, but for a shorter future
    Than I imagined.

EDWIN: Brief, and getting briefer.

TATA: We are past danger now, the worst has happened.
    Could we just die?

EDWIN: How is it done, I wonder?

LILLA: Come quickly! Woden carries us away on
    his whirlwind; I will whirl my swords, I will duck
    and run!

EDWIN: Nothing will save us.

TATA: I depend on it.

EDWIN: I will not pray, or sacrifice to Woden.

TATA: I will keep faith, and sacrifice to nothing.

LILLA: Woden! Run! Woden!

Exeunt different ways.

Scene 6

The battle of Chester. Enter ANEIRIN leading OLWEN who has blinded herself.

OLWEN: I tore my eyes out not to see this happen.
    But I can hear it as I heard my mother
    Crying to bring me out into the daylight.
    What do you see?

ANEIRIN: The army of the English,
    Hiding a hill. Our army in the valley
    Strung out. And I can see King Ethelfrith,
    His helmet is a raven with glass eyes,
    And he is pointing at another hill
    Where all our monks and bishops are assembled
    Praying against him, crying out to heaven
    To send down madness on the Englishmen
    So that they turn and slaughter one another.

OLWEN: What was that shout?

ANEIRIN: A troop of Englishmen
    Has broken out of the main body and
    Crossed to the hill on which our holy men
    Are stationed undefended. And the arms
    Rising and falling, of the Englishmen –
    It is as if the monks were planks of pine
    Being cut short and hammered to a frame
    To make a little house. The heathens roar,
    And the whole hillside slips into the valley!

OLWEN: We will be better as a memory,
    We leave the English only earth and stone,
    The world is theirs, the weather is our kingdom.
    It was a sad life having to pretend
    To be substantial, now the joke is over,
    Our death has ended, we are in the kingdom,
    Out of our people's carcase larks are rising!

Enter WARRIORS. They drag off OLWEN.

ACT FOUR

Scene 1

The court of KING RAEDWALD of the East Angles. Enter EDWIN.

EDWIN: We ran like wolves, and King Ethelfrith's foxhounds yelped with a hysterical note. And we changed into salmon and swam upstream through time and leapt into the belly of a heron that shadowed the land with its wings to the fens and the court of King Raedwald of the East Angles. King Ethelbert is dead, so is Augustine. And here I am, the dead leaf on the stream. I find I have confused myself with other people in my memories, I have passed through so many hands. Was it I or someone else who started a new religion in Kent with the king's daughter? I think it must have been me, or a tramp I met on the road – but then that was probably me too. Oh Tata, priestess of emptiness! Now I am the pope of nothing. I was zero, when I understood that I would never see you again. Now I am much less. How can I stem the wound, stop this emptying? Simple – sit down, never move again.

Enter LILLA.

LILLA: My Lord, run!

EDWIN: What? Is it necessary? Won't whatever it is wait till we get to it?

LILLA: Escape!

EDWIN: Oh escape! Run away, you mean, not towards. Why?

LILLA: Oh my Lord, don't try to make jokes. It has happened again. Only quicker this time.

EDWIN: Of course.

LILLA: Ethelfrith's ambassadors have offered King
　　Raedwald so much that he has finally caved in,
　　they've scooped his guts out and stuffed him full
　　of money –

EDWIN: Money for Edwin. I wonder how much.

LILLA: They'll take you today without warning and
　　hand you over to Ethelfrith.

EDWIN: I will be glad to see the king. I don't know
　　what it is he's been wanting to tell me all these
　　years. Perhaps I left something behind.

LILLA: No, you definitely left everything. Where shall
　　we go?

EDWIN: That's a good question! Scotland? Been there.
　　Mercia, same – Wales – Wessex, Kent –

LILLA: We could cross the sea to Gaul.

EDWIN: No.

LILLA: Why not?

EDWIN: I can't be bothered.

LILLA: Then you'll die.

EDWIN: Well, it's time.

LILLA: Oh pull yourself together! Start screaming!

EDWIN: I'm not running away this time.

LILLA: Then run towards something.

EDWIN: I've got this bit of grit in my shoe and I can't
　　be bothered to take the shoe off, do you know what
　　I mean? But it puts walking out of the question. You
　　say King Raedwald wants to sell me to Ethelfrith.

Very well, I believe your intelligence. But I will
not dishonour my friend Raedwald by acting as if
I believed he would do such a thing.

LILLA: But you do believe that he will do it?

EDWIN: Yes, if you say so.

LILLA: Then act on your belief!

EDWIN: No.

LILLA: This is madness. This is Woden. I have seen
this happen to men in battle, suddenly they just
freeze. It is Woden.

EDWIN: I am the master of my own movements, for the
moment, and I decide not to move, not in the present.

LILLA: For the sake of a friendship that doesn't exist!

EDWIN: They are the most common kind.

LILLA: Ah Woden, release him! I have sacrificed to
you enough!

EDWIN: That's what I am, a sacrifice to Woden.

LILLA gets down on his hands and knees and grazes.

EDWIN: What are you doing?

LILLA: Who?

EDWIN: Get up!

LILLA: I will go to the court, and throw myself at the
king's feet.

EDWIN: If you like. Thank you, Lilla.

Exit LILLA.

Tata, if we had ever been together, this would have
happened many times. You believe the worst of

those you love. But you try to stand fast like an
oak in the night storm of that faith. When you
hear of my death, you will think, how squalid,
he was dragged off and carried north, shouted at
a bit and then stabbed in the back of the neck.
You won't know how I stood fast on the stream
of my friend's love, walked on that lake. Ah! Here
they come!

Enter an ANGEL. EDWIN jumps up.

Who are you? Are you Woden in disguise?
Are you a friend of Christ? Forgive my rambling,
I am half mad, my good, true friend the king
Has just betrayed me, and the double-vision
Required to see both sides of his devotion
Makes the world blurred to me. My poor old mind.

ANGEL: Edwin, you are at the extremity
　　　Where earth and heaven meet. It is not true
　　　That at the end there is no help for men.
　　　Edwin, for you the end has not yet come.
　　　You are to be the greatest king in Britain.

EDWIN: Not me!

ANGEL:　　　　To rule a kingdom made of kingdoms.
　　　All races in this island will acknowledge
　　　Your sovereignty.

EDWIN:　　　　　That is impossible.

ANGEL: But tell me this. If what I say came true,
　　　Would you accept the guidance of the spirit
　　　Who told you that these things would be?

EDWIN:　　　　　　　　　That prophet
　　　Would never lose my faith, depend on it
　　　Utterly!

ANGEL:　When the things I prophesy
　　　Have happened, Edwin, listen to the man
　　　Who gives you this sign.

He puts his hand on EDWIN's head.

> That will be the one
> In whom the spirit of this truth is living.
> Remember this, and if you trust in me,
> When all these things have happened, trust in him,
> And he will show you how to make your kingdom
> An everlasting heavenly example.

Exit ANGEL.

EDWIN: Now I am just imaginary.

Enter LILLA.

LILLA: My Lord!

EDWIN: No need to run away now, Lilla, I've disappeared.

LILLA: No need to run away, you're right there.

EDWIN: I am God.

LILLA: Edwin! The king has changed his mind!

EDWIN: Yes, I know that.

LILLA: No – changed it again! His wife the queen likes you, she screamed at him, she brought him to his knees, he can't believe what he was about to do, he curses Ethelfrith for making him even consider it, and he has sent this message: King Ethelfrith, not only will I not hand over to you Edwin, my friend, for any amount of avarice, but I swear by Woden and Thor that I will march against you this day and put King Edwin on his rightful throne.

EDWIN: King Edwin!

LILLA: My Lord, it will happen!

EDWIN: Well, we'll see!

Exeunt.

Scene 2

The court of King Eadbald. Enter PAULINUS and TATA. BERTHA lies asleep in a bed.

TATA: You will become my mother after her.
  Are you prepared for that?

PAULINUS: I will attempt it.
  But more exactly, I will be your chaplain.

TATA: It will not be promotion. You have been
  The chaplain of a queen, but as for me,
  Since I am not my father's son and heir,
  And he is dead, my place has disappeared.

PAULINUS: You are yourself, and that is all I ask for.

TATA: You are a true friend, and the truth deserves you.
  I have a strange confession. I have gone
  To church each Sunday since I was a child,
  And prayed beside my mother, drunk the wine,
  Eaten the bread – but I am not a Christian.
  I know Christ's heart, I understand his doctrine,
  But simply I do not believe in him.
  I am alone on earth, and my request
  Is that you will not speak about religion
  After my mother, but remain my friend.
  Don't tell me that her soul has gone to heaven,
  I will not listen. Let me turn to stone
  When she is dead. You see how much I trust you.

PAULINUS: And Tata, I will not abandon you.
  Though if your ears are well and truly closed,
  You must allow me time to work elsewhere;
  Archbishop Laurence is a man for kings,
  Which leaves the people stormbound by their dreams.
  So let me give them half my time, and you
  All of the rest, in honour of your mother.

TATA: Why is it that the truest love affairs
　　　Take place in absence? Why is it the case
　　　That when my heart beats hardest for that man
　　　I am with someone else, or on my own,
　　　Complaining to a friend or to the wall?

PAULINUS: Pity the priest, who longs for God on earth.
　　　We are apart till death us do connect.

TATA: This is our best connection – you and I
　　　Are both in absence, waiting for another.
　　　Edwin is dead: I mean, he is the king.
　　　For two years he has ruled Northumbria
　　　In glory and he has not called for me.
　　　I am just getting ready to be nothing,
　　　But my heart stamps its foot and blows its trumpet
　　　For its friend Edwin, and my dreams demand him.

PAULINUS: And I believe that he will send for you.

TATA: No, it would have to be a miracle.
　　　Then everything would be believable.

　　　BERTHA stirs. They go over to her.

BERTHA: Now Tata, you must tell the king your father
　　　I need to see him. It has been too long
　　　Since he and I spoke sweetly to each other.
　　　Ethelbert, sweetheart, I was only joking,
　　　It was a saltpot, all those years of anger,
　　　Containing sugar – swapped for no good reason,
　　　But in the end we tasted one another.
　　　Tata, forgive me, I am disappearing.
　　　But I had hoped that there was news of Edwin.

TATA: No news of him.

BERTHA:　　　　　　　I heard you say his name.

　　　Enter LILLA.

LILLA: Tata! Tata!

PAULINUS: Hush, the queen is dying.

LILLA: No – ! Look, I can't hush, priest, I've trudged all the way from Northumbria and it rained every day. Things have been happening, friend – I'm sorry about the queen but I'm dying to tell you about them –

TATA: Lilla, be quiet. Whatever your news, it can't be more important than the end of my mother's life.

LILLA: Oh yes it can. Who cares about the end? The end can take care of itself, it's the middle you've got to worry about. Tata! Tata! How have you been?

TATA: My father is dead, my mother is dying, Edwin I haven't seen.

LILLA: Things have been going extremely well with him. You must have heard –

TATA: One or two things.

LILLA: Ethelfrith is dead. Now it's King Edwin.

TATA: Well done.

LILLA: He's getting married. That's what I came to tell you.

TATA: Wonderful. I hope he will be very happy.

LILLA: He has stamped out Ethelfrith and all his followers, so now he has decided to settle down.

TATA: He must have been very busy. Now, if you don't mind, my mother is dying.

LILLA: But don't you even want to know who the bride is?

TATA: Dear God, I don't care if it's the Queen of the Turks and she's had fifteen husbands and poisoned the lot of them. I don't care if it's Maude with six teeth and a broomstick, I don't care if it's a stuffed cat, I don't care if it's a bloody spider in socks, he

can marry whoever he likes and I'll dance and laugh
and sing till I'm sick.

LILLA: My master Edwin has regained his kingdom,
    And he wants you to be his wife and queen.
    Do you agree?

TATA: I do.

PAULINUS: A miracle!

TATA: Of slowness, yes – a creeping miracle.

LILLA: He's sorry he took so long. But being a king is
    very bewildering for him. Now he's found his feet
    and he knows what he wants: you.

BERTHA: I thought I heard that. You were wrong to
                              hide it.
    Rejoice and die. But listen to me, Tata.
    He is a pagan, your betrothed; you love him,
    Or so you say – but Tata, learn from me;
    Do not be stubborn and deny yourself
    To him to force him to become a Christian.
    All marriages are sacred in God's eyes,
    You can be one without the force of doctrine,
    The wall that stood between this man and me
    Was not put up by love but by impatience –
    Whatever law commands you under heaven
    Other than love, despise it and refuse it.
    And so I push you from my womb again,
    With a great cry, but that I keep inside.

TATA: Mother, I will not keep him off, believe me.

BERTHA: Then I am glad to let you go, my darling.
    I go from south to north, and leave the world,
    Heading without direction to the next one.
    Following signposts you might lose your way,
    But I will guide you if you pray to me.
    Goodbye, Paulinus, be our Lord to her.

I am returning to the conversation
That I was having with the king my husband.

TATA: Mother, goodbye! That you and he will lie
In the same tomb, is God's best gift to me.

Exeunt all but TATA.

TATA: Now she is dead – which bangs a black lid down
On the bright news that filled my head just now.
I am a coffin stuffed with wedding flowers,
My mother's death is an ascent in satin
Through storms of roses – so the mind confuses
Separate issues that are thrown together
By time that crams. But why it has to happen
That after such a lengthy stretch of nothing
This death should be contained in this proposal,
Who knows? Not me, I only know the stretching
Takes a long time, but then the snap is sudden,
And the same tether held me to my mother,
Her to this world, and me to Kent. It breaks,
And she flies up, and I fly north to Edwin.

Exit.

ACT FIVE

Scene 1

A mountain in Northumbria. Enter NORTHUMBRIANS laughing and crying. Some clap and beat a merry drumbeat, while others beat their breasts and weep and tear their clothing. They are escorting a YOUNG MAN, who walks semi-naked wearing a crown and a purple cloak. A PRIEST follows with a garotte. The 'MOURNERS' and 'CELEBRATORS' form a circle around him. The beat turns into a steady one as the PRIEST approaches the SACRIFICE from behind, and then suddenly stops.

PRIEST: To you, Woden, and to this mountain, and to the sky and to the eagle in the sun and all streams that run through rocks to the sea and to all foreign gods and gods with no name, we the grass offer our flower. For the life you give, we give you our king! Oh have mercy on us!

The drumbeats build to a crescendo. The PRIEST is about to kill the SACRIFICE. Enter PAULINUS. Everyone suddenly stops and turns to him.

PAULINUS: Northumbrians, why have you stopped what you were doing?

PRIEST: Carry on!

1ST NORTHUMBRIAN: Not while he is here!

PAULINUS: Why should I stop you?

2ND NORTHUMBRIAN: Paulinus, go away, you have no part of this.

PAULINUS: Are you ashamed?

3RD NORTHUMBRIAN: We are not as strong as you. That is why we do this.

83

PAULINUS: My friends, I am no stronger than you are. Look, I am worn out from walking up this mountain, and if you look at my foot you will see a clear sign that I am not a god. I walked all the way from Rome to the English sea and from Thanet to Canterbury and here but your mountains are more than a match for me.

2ND NORTHUMBRIAN: I'll wash your feet.

PAULINUS: Oh you angel!

2ND NORTHUMBRIAN washes PAULINUS' feet.

PRIEST: But then you must leave us. Though you are able to live without sacrifice, we are not.

PAULINUS: You are wrong. You and I are no different.

PRIEST: What is your sacrifice?

PAULINUS: Mine has been done once and for all. Consider this: if God is God, then there is nothing better than God. So what could be a sacrifice to God except God himself?

PRIEST: As Woden hanged himself on the tree.

PAULINUS: As I say, you are no different from me, not in the slightest way.

1ST NORTHUMBRIAN: Are you saying that you believe in our religion?

PAULINUS: Absolutely.

PRIEST: We give what is given to us.

PAULINUS: So do I.

PRIEST: And what is that?

PAULINUS: More than life.

NORTHUMBRIANS: What is it?

1ST NORTHUMBRIAN: The king!

Enter EDWIN and LILLA.

LILLA: I know who told you this prophecy – it was Woden! He peered down and saw, like a beacon, the soul of Edwin blazing, and next to him his faithful servant, who through all his years of vicissitude and memory loss, stood by him.

PAULINUS: King Edwin!

EDWIN: Stand up! Stand up! Forgive me, priests, for hunting on your holy mountain.

PRIEST: King Edwin, listen to my petition! We came here to make our spring sacrifice. If you still believe in the teachings of your fathers, King, I ask you to send this man away, who has stopped our spring sacrifice –

EDWIN: I cannot send him away. I have said that he can teach in my kingdom.

PRIEST: Then how shall I perform the sacrifice?

EDWIN: If no-one will do it with you, you must do it on your own.

PRIEST: Will you join me?

EDWIN: Not today.

PRIEST: Who will stay to perform this sacrifice?

1ST NORTHUMBRIAN: Set him free!

They untie the SACRIFICE and burst out laughing and dancing.

PAULINUS: People, I must speak to the king. Go back to the village. I will join you.

Exeunt NORTHUMBRIANS.

LILLA: My Lord, you will die!

EDWIN: I suppose so.

LILLA: Too soon!

EDWIN: I want to speak to Paulinus.

LILLA: Then I leave you. Woden! Forgive this ingratitude! I will watch from the big rock, and I only hope I don't drop it on his head.

Exit LILLA.

PAULINUS: What is your trouble?

EDWIN: Paulinus, you have found your place. You have set your foot on the king of all hills. I know that you do not want to waste your time on kings; but all men are naked on the mountain, all are the same, and perhaps by climbing I have earned a little of you.

PAULINUS: King, what is troubling you?

EDWIN: Something very strange happened. Which was, as it turned out, a divine event – something you ought to know about. And this is my question: can nothing keep us together? In a high wind, does nothing break like an oak, or does it bend?

PAULINUS: King, your religion is beyond me –

EDWIN: I ought to be able to speak straight now. Something has given me victory. Something. A vision told me all that would happen. But I have sworn to Tata to believe in nothing.

PAULINUS: A vision!

EDWIN: So you see I have to lie, but she can tell, and she hates me. I have been an exile. I can tell four

o'clock from half past four by the shape of a smile.
This is the position that my victory has placed me in
– worse than exile. Exile from her. And now a child
is coming! I know this – I am nothing but Tata-love.
If you cut me open you'd find nothing but her, heaps
of her, millions of little Tatas running about. It is
agony for me to believe anything she doesn't believe!

PAULINUS: It will be easier when you have a child –

EDWIN: Why?

PAULINUS: You won't see so much of her.

EDWIN: Priest, I sentence you to death!

PAULINUS: I submit to your judgement. Tata! Your
love is all fear! God help us.

EDWIN: What god?

PAULINUS: The god who sent this revelation. Your
god and my God, never mind the name.

EDWIN: This was all I wanted, to speak these words to
you, here on the mountain. Now I must go. Thank
you, priest, for listening to this king.

Exit EDWIN.

PAULINUS: God give me grace; the Crown has come
to me,
When I had started with the earth beneath it.

Enter TATA, pregnant.

PAULINUS: Tata!

TATA: My hermit on the holy mountain!

PAULINUS: My dear, this child is ready to be born,
What are you doing out of your bedchamber,
How did you get here?

TATA: Oh, my maids obey me
When they observe a certain look in my eye.

PAULINUS: At least the king is hunting on this
mountain.

TATA: I had to see you, and I am the queen.
I only want to talk about my mother!
You are the only person here who loved her;
I miss my mother!

PAULINUS: I remember her
In all my prayers – a being of pure fire.

TATA: I am all earth, and I have need of her.

PAULINUS: What are you saying?

TATA: Pagan priests delight
To talk about the future of the world,
When everything disintegrates in flames –
But what about my future? To be torn
By a black dragon jammed between my bones!
And I must face all this without my mother!

PAULINUS: My child –

TATA: Be silent! You are just a man
Like God or Woden; you know everything
But nothing that means anything to me.
If I survive the imp's escape, what then?
As my poor daughter or my son grows taller,
How shall I teach it what it is? It is
An invitation I would not accept
That I extend to this unborn confusion:
O come to earth and live with us and die,
Without once knowing what you are or why.
Give me my mother!

PAULINUS: She is here with us,
As close as Christ.

TATA: My mother came to me
   Faintly at dawn – she said she wants to be
   Beside me when the final shudder comes,
   But that she cannot find me in the spheres;
   The one that I have chosen is the one
   That no-one else can reach.

PAULINUS: You saw your mother...

TATA: Whether it was my mother or a dream,
   I know that she is not dead, not like stone!
   Why are these words that should be heard by Edwin
   The one thing that I cannot say to him?
   You must not tell him!

She has a contraction.

PAULINUS: Women! Any women?
   The hunt is coming back.

TATA: You must not tell him!
   Swear not to tell him I am on the mountain.

Enter maids in waiting, who take off TATA

PAULINUS: God, this is very strange! What are you
   doing? What are you doing?

Enter EUMER.

EUMER: Friend, is it true that King Edwin is on
   this mountain?

PAULINUS: That is his hunt coming.

EUMER: I am a messenger from the King of Wessex.
   My name is Eumer. We were travelling to his palace,
   but since we have met him, would you announce me
   to him?

PAULINUS: Yes I will, Eumer.

Enter EDWIN and LORDS.

EDWIN: Where are those women? Where are
those women?

PAULINUS: King! Eumer, an ambassador from the
King of Wessex!

EDWIN: Strange place to meet you, Eumer. But it will
do. Welcome.

LILLA: I swear a moment ago he was a group
of women.

EUMER: King Edwin! I thank you for granting me an
audience among the eagles. I have no wish to interrupt
your hunting, but the urgency of my message and the
honour of him who sends me fill me with courage. My
message from King Cuichelm is this – for Ethelfrith –
vengeance!

*He lunges at EDWIN with a dagger. LILLA intervenes and
is run through. The dagger-point wounds EDWIN through
LILLA's body. The LORDS cry out and cut down EUMER,
who goes down fighting, growling like a bear.*

EDWIN: Lilla!

1ST LORD: Dead!

LILLA: No, no – nearly.

EDWIN: Lilla! You saved me! You threw yourself
between –

LILLA: No, I tripped.

EDWIN: You stepped.

LILLA: Well, I stepped. But it was just a joke. Not
my best.

EDWIN: You who gave me this kingdom, save him! He
is my follower, I vouch for him.

LILLA: King, listen, this is how it is. We don't know
anything about anything. It's like we're in a hall on
a windy night and the doors are open at either end
and in flies a sparrow and you see it for a moment
in the firelight then it's out again into the rain. We
can't see where it came from, we can't see where it's
going. Woden, be satisfied with my last sacrifice.
And my last word is this – baaaaa, baaaaa.

Dies.

EDWIN: Bless you, Lilla! Lilla, listen, Lilla! I'm the
king but I can't make him listen.

1ST LORD: You are wounded, King. The dagger
was poisoned.

EDWIN: Lilla! The last one! Lilla!

2ND LORD: You must get medicine, King, this dagger
was poisoned.

EDWIN: No, I think I'm alright. It hit an unimportant
part I think, an unnecessary memory. Take Lilla
away. Goodbye, my friend. That was true love,
he stood in the way. Did you see that? He did,
didn't he?

2ND LORD: He did, King, we all saw it.

1ST LORD: No-one will ever forget!

EDWIN: Or did he trip?

3RD LORD: No, he stepped!

EDWIN: Paulinus, this is your moment. Tell
me something.

PAULINUS: I am sorry, until my God explains this to
me, I have nothing to say.

He puts his hand on EDWIN's head and withdraws it.

EDWIN: Put it back.

PAULINUS: Forgive me, King, I was carried away. For a moment I thought you were one of your subjects.

EDWIN: Do that again.

PAULINUS: What?

EDWIN: Do what you did again.

PAULINUS puts his hand back on his head.

EDWIN: Listen to the man that gives you this sign.
I think my mind is affecting the poison. Somewhere a toad is turning in its grave. My God. My God!

Enter TATA followed by distressed maids.

TATA: Edwin.

MAID: My Lord, my Lady, please! – she heard that you are wounded –

EDWIN: Tata! We have a child!

TATA: You were calling to god.

EDWIN: Tata, forgive me. It is in the open.
But I have never moved my eyes away
From your eyes, though the lying cracked my brain!

TATA: What have you seen?

EDWIN: An angel came to me –

TATA: An angel?

EDWIN: At King Raedwald's court, and told me
That I would win the kingdom of my father.

TATA: Why did you hide this from me?

EDWIN: And he gave me
    A sign and told me to believe whoever
    Gave it again.

TATA: Is this delirium?

EDWIN: My love, today, Paulinus gave the sign.

TATA: I did not know that I had been abandoned,
    Though I suspected that the end was coming –
    Now I know why – because my love was lying!

EDWIN: God of disaster! God of mayhem!

*EDWIN and TATA start to exit separate ways. The MAID
gives TATA the child.*

PAULINUS: Wait! We are standing on a holy mountain,
    Do not run off like angry bishops, cursing,
    Calling damnation down on one another,
    Swearing to stick to your extremes forever.
    Before you turn your hearts to stone, consider
    The ground you stamp on. I was born in Rome,
    And I have kissed the earth which Paul and Peter
    Drenched with their deaths, but I have never known
    A place as full of angels as this island,
    That lies wide open to the light of heaven.
    Oh claim this power for yourselves, my children.

Exit PAULINUS.

EDWIN: So we must try to speak to one another.

TATA: Where was your courage, when you hid from me?

EDWIN: Hiding in you, too deep for me to find.

TATA: You mean your faith made you afraid of me?

EDWIN: All I could offer was a mystery.

TATA: I was no longer everything to you.

EDWIN: A truth impossible for love to say.

TATA: But love must say exactly what it means.

EDWIN: Tata, my love is wider than the sky.

TATA: Your love for heaven or your love for me?

EDWIN: You are my love – that is for you to say.

TATA: I wish that nothing was the truth, my friend!
    Then you and I would be the same forever
    As when we started, and admit no others!
    But then, another has already come,
    And we must break our hearts to let her in.
    And who will help us make them whole again?
    I see that since Paulinus gave the sign,
    It binds you to him.

EDWIN: You must not deny
    What you believe for any love of me
    That has survived my cowardice and lies.

TATA: But when I look into the dark, I find
    The moon is Edwin and the stars are Edwin.
    And it is simple. I must sacrifice
    Nothing or Edwin. So now nothing dies.

Enter PAULINUS. TATA gives the child to him.

PAULINUS: We stand before the reason and the cause,
    Who speaks of love in many languages,
    Through monks and lovers and the rain and wind;
    These are the words of God, who will not stop them
    For loss of faith in us.

EDWIN: We two have brought you
    Our child to be protected by your blessing,
    In recognition of this mystery:
    That she is us, but also something new,
    And that has come from nothing we can see.

PAULINUS: So follow if you can the lead she gives you.
    Only as children can we reach the kingdom.
    Dear God, I give you Eanfled, the daughter
    Of Tata and of Edwin. Make her yours,
    And give her grace to be her parents' teacher.

    I place you, Eanfled, on the mountain. In the name
    of the Father, the Son and the Holy Spirit, I baptise
    you Eanfled. Amen.

    Exeunt.

Scene 2

Enter ANEIRIN and TATA with a child in her arms.

ANEIRIN: These people took their passion, that had
                              blown
    Towards the edge of chaos, to Christ's throne,
    And there it changed into a deathless diamond,
    Cage of the sun, that shone throughout their kingdom.
    But then one Christian and one pagan king
    Allied against King Edwin, fought and killed him.
    Queen Tata, tearless on the English shore,
    Cried out to Christ to keep her spirit clear.
    And it was made eternal on that day;
    She did not curse her god; she turned to him.
    But my own people died into the little hills
    And broke across the back of woods like winds
                             that rain.
    And you can hear them from the evening until dawn;
    The ghosts of Britain gather on the cliffs to sing
    Back at the waves that heap up moonlight on the shore,
    Where Caesar's legions leap into the spear-cut foam;
    The insubstantial battle wavers all night long
    But when the sun gets up the war of ghosts gives place
    To battles in the shallows of the present moment.

Song sung by all cast, one verse each and then all singing the last verse.

The place once known as Albion
Now known as Britain, is an island
Not far from Belgium in the ocean,
Not far from France, and quite near Holland.

Which on the other side receives
The sea that has no other side,
And oak and ash and other leaves
Gather and scatter on the tide.

Oh there are vines and there is corn,
And horses walking on the land,
Dry timber ready to be sawn,
And salmon heavy in the hand.

Various types of birds abound
On sea and land, and on the shore;
And there are dolphins to be found
Close in, and I can tell you more:

Shellfish and oysters, hard and light
Are sometimes found containing pearls,
Violet, green, but mainly white,
God's promise in the ears of girls.

Whelks are abundant, and a dye
Is got from them that lasts forever,
Deep scarlet like the evening sky
That prophesies angelic weather –

It actually improves with age.
This country is alive with flowers,
Like clematis and saxifrage,
Glorying in the frequent showers.

There are at present in these islands,
Four nations: English, British, Irish
And Picts. The Picts are in the highlands.
And with God's help we all shall flourish.